the political theory of local government

W. Hardy Wickwar

Ir618

the political theory of local government

university of south carolina press
columbia, south carolina

FIRST EDITION
Copyright © 1970 by
THE UNIVERSITY OF SOUTH CAROLINA PRESS

Published in Columbia, S.C., by the
University of South Carolina Press, 1970

Standard Book Number: 87249-174-9

Library of Congress Catalog Card Number: 71-95258

Manufactured in the United States of America by
Kingsport Press, Inc., Kingsport, Tennessee

Designed by Robert L. Nance

preface

the dynamism of what is now the developed quarter
of the world has many institutional aspects. Among them
is a type of state that the world had not previously
seen, in that the dimensions of its territory and population might approach those of an ancient empire, whereas
the civic participation of its people has recalled that of
an ancient city state. In this unprecedented kind of state,
Local Government has been an essential link between
the central government and the people, and one of the
characteristics therefore of all the states that have made
the modern world.

Local Government has evolved, moreover, along with
the evolution of government as a whole. To each phase

in the evolution of the modern state, there is a corresponding phase in the evolution of its Local Government. One of the themes of this study is thus the succession of several well-marked phases in this constantly evolving relationship.

Its second theme is that what distinguishes each of these successive phases is a characteristic way of thinking, and that the disentangling of these different thought-patterns is helpful to us today in clarifying our current approaches to the role and place of Local Government in the contemporary state.

A third theme is that the diffusion of the state system of the Atlantic countries into the rest of the world has included a multiform diffusion of Local Government and that these new local institutions reflect a range of different ideas. This study then becomes a comparative study of local government theory relative to place as well as time.

Since we are studying a culture trait that has always been transnational and is now becoming worldwide, some familiar phenomena appear here in an unfamiliar context and perspective, which may be different from the setting in which they would be found if the focus were essentially national.

Since Local Government, like all public administration in the modern state, is essentially a creature of law, its political theory has been to a large extent identical with its legal philosophy. It is, therefore, with the evolving legal philosophy of Local Government that we are here mainly concerned; the evidence for this philosophy is to be found to some extent in legislation and judicial decision, but above all in the philosophizing of jurists, legal historians, and law reformers.

My thinking about these problems began in 1937 with a course of lectures on local government and social service delivered at the London School of Economics and Political Science at the invitation of Harold Laski. It advanced from 1952 during ten years' preoccupation with United Nations aid to local community development, broken in 1961 with a year at the American University of Beirut where the first draft of this book was exposed to the reactions of students of many nationalities. Some of the threads that have been woven into it have already been used in the *International Review of Administrative Sciences,* the International Institute of Local Authorities *Quarterly,* the *Middle East Journal,* Professor F. Morstein Marx's *Foreign Governments,* and, anonymously and cooperatively, in United Nations publications, to all of which I am grateful for an opportunity to develop views which they have not necessarily shared.

Lieber College
University of South Carolina
September 1969

contents

the political theory of local government

1

an intermediary body

Is Local Government self-government, or is it a creature of the state?

These antithetical positions run through the whole evolution of modern local government theory. They may be traced back to Western Europe's middle ages, when a tradition evolved of local liberties being in practice self-achieved, but when also this tradition was soon overshadowed by a legal doctrine of local bodies being incorporated by the sovereign. They may be traced back also to the emergence of the early modern state, when a new classical political theory hesitated between thinking of local bodies as quasi-sovereign constituents of the state or as subordinate intermediary bodies between the

sovereign and his subjects. It is in these antecedents and
alternatives, and in the ways in which men expressed
themselves when elaborating them, that the roots of local
government theory are to be found.

local liberties

Boroughs and communes arose spontaneously in
Western Christendom between 1050 and 1250, without
any one giving much thought to theory. They arose because the inhabitants of certain localities wanted various
"liberties" that would give them greater privileges than
feudal lords allowed to manorial villages. These franchises related particularly to the use of their property and
included a land-tenure that would approximate to free-
hold; toll-free access to a yearly fair as well as a weekly
market; the "farm" of the revenue hitherto collected by
their lord's reeve; the exemption of their persons from
being treated as a form of property; a wall and belfry, so
as to defend their liberties against armed attack; a court
in which to apply their customs and ordinances; officers
of their own choosing to manage these common interests;
and immunity from outside interference in their affairs.

The emphasis might vary, from civilian English concern
with land-tenure and revenue-farming to militant French
interest in a sworn mutual-aid covenant for the local
maintenance of armed peace. Everywhere, however, and
with such means and weapons as they could muster,
burghers reached agreement with their lord on the extent
of their local liberties and franchises, and then set these
down in a charter for him to seal. Like all customary
status defined by written charter in the middle ages, and
like feudalism itself, the relationship between a borough
or commune and its lord was thus to some extent con-
tractual or at least consensual. It is thus in terms of
contemporary practice, precedent and procedure, rather
than of general legal theory, that the emergence of medieval urban liberties has to be understood.

chartered corporations

Theory first became important with the revival of
Roman law from about 1250. Hitherto, no one had asked
whether a borough or commune was an aggregate of
individuals or a body corporate. Now, however, this became an important question. It began to be said that the
possession of a common chest, a common seal, a belfry,
or a townhall, in perpetual succession, meant that the
group must be a body corporate (*universitas*). It could
now sue and be sued in the person of its mayor, rather
than as a group of individuals. It was held, moreover, that
this legal personality was something that had not grown
naturally, but had been artificially created by the sovereign; the body corporate was a *persona ficta*. A charter
now came to be envisaged as an act of incorporation,
granted unilaterally by the ruler. This concept distinguished the chartered corporation, on the one hand, from
an entirely self-constituted association or partnership
(*societas*) and, on the other, from Christendom, which
also was a corporate body (*universitas*) but one that was
instituted by divine rather than human law.

This theory of incorporation, moreover, was deeply
influenced by the concept of the foundation, that is to
say, an undying body of patrons incorporated in order
that they might manage a perpetual endowment in the
interest of a specified clientele. The body incorporated
tended, therefore, to be not the commonalty or community at large, but its collegial organ: the municipality was
henceforward the mayor and council, and not the burgesses. Justification was thus found for power in the
incorporated communities to be concentrated in the
hands of select bodies, which endeavored to pass it on
by becoming self-perpetuating "close corporations." This
meant particularly power over corporate property, power
to decide who were to benefit from it as burgesses, and
power to designate representatives of the local community to a national parliamentary "community of com-

munities" (*communitas communitatum*) such as the English house of commons or the French third estate.

Another consequence of these doctrines was that the sovereign could exercise power over local bodies by means of the granting, revision, or revocation of charters. To some extent, charters of explicit incorporation were granted; to some extent, however, this was a matter of legal construction, with jurists assuming that local bodies were implicitly incorporated if they farmed their own revenue. In any case, the local body was brought into subjection to the sovereign. Henceforward the charter was a grant rather than a contract. Instead of freeing local bodies from outside interference, the charter now exposed them to it. To this reinterpretation of local privileges, the patrician ruling families of the boroughs and communes made but little objection; for this was the age when mercantilism was dawning, as a policy that based the wealth of the merchants on the power of the state, and the power of the state on the wealth of the merchants.

from free city to princely state

While this process of state-formation was occurring in England and France, a different reaction to Roman-law doctrine occurred in the Rhineland. During the period 1250–1550, the emperor here failed to build on the claim of court lawyers that the corporate character of local bodies depended on his will, while these local bodies, on the other hand, accepted his nominal authority only on condition that he should not exercise it. "Imperial cities" thus became "free cities"; and free communities, usually urban but occasionally rural, banded together in armed regional defense leagues, of which two were to survive as the Swiss Confederation and the United Provinces of the Low Countries.

For most German cities, however, subordination to the ruler was only delayed and, when at last it arrived, was to occur in the different and much stricter form of absolute subjection to a number of territorial princes rather than subordinate cooperation with the one national emperor. The liberties of all but the greatest of them were eventually eclipsed during the wars of religion of 1618–48, when territorial principalities alone proved able to assure the peace which burghers needed; the most flourishing cities in the German states were henceforward the new princely capitals, which owed their well-ordered prosperity to the ruler's residence among them. To cameralist professors training administrators in the princes' new state universities, cities were to be ruled, rather than to rule themselves; they were state-instituted, rather than self-constituted. To professors of public law, the state was the patrimony of the ruler, and cities were but part of his domain, much as in classical Roman law they had been subject oligarchies on the public domain of the sovereign Roman state.

local communities as components of the eary modern state

It was in these years 1550–1650 that the legal and political theory of the modern state was to have its beginning. Being preoccupied with the new phenomenon of sovereign power, one of the questions that concerned the founders of the new legal and political theory in England, France, and the Low Countries was the relationship between the new state and the lesser groups that came within its orbit.

Early-modern classical theorists in these countries could not be content with reading Roman law into a non-Roman situation. Instead, they had to take account of a certain reciprocity, a certain two-way traffic of power and influence, that was inherent in the life of the medieval and early-modern West European kingdoms as it never had been in that of the Roman empire. Boroughs and counties were represented in the house of commons; communes were represented—and by Bodin among others—in the third estate; and no new taxes could be levied on them without their consent. Subject though they might be to the sovereign, they thus had a constitutional relationship to him such as had never been achieved by local bodies in antiquity. The first adumbration of true local government theory therefore begins with the first consciousness of this distinctive relationship.

Nor could the early classical theorists be content with medieval moral and legal philosophy. In their preoccupation with the divine institution of Christendom, medieval schoolmen had given surprisingly little attention to the everyday forms of group life that were flourishing around them. With the shift in focus from Christendom as a whole to the individual states into which it was being organized, the traditional distinction between good and tyrannical rulers became reinforced in the fifteenth century with the conception of the good ruler as one who associated with him the estates of the realm including the burghers; and by the late sixteenth century this conception of the articulated state had broadened in North-West Europe to take account explicitly of the interaction between the ruler and local communities as well as other collective entities. This evolution could of course be completed only in those countries where cities were now embraced within a wider state, instead of dominating it as in the Italy of the Renaissance.

There were, however, two ways of interpreting this new relationship between the all-inclusive state and the lesser communities contained within it. Did these subject lesser bodies owe their survival to sovereign power? Or were they the sovereign source from which power originated? The former assumption was that of Bodin in France; the latter was that of Althusius in the Low Countries.

intermediary bodies

In France and England there was now no doubt as to the subordination of chartered local corporations to the sovereign. The only question was as to the degree of their remaining liberty. This proved important enough to give support to a theory that flourished from Bodin to Montesquieu and found general acceptance among political theorists for two hundred years, except to some extent in the German states. This was the theory of "intermediary bodies."

Jean Bodin's *Six Bookes of a Commonweale* was published in 1576 in French and in 1606 in English. Within fifty years it had gone through eighteen editions in French, Latin, Italian, Spanish, and English before undergoing a revival in the mid-eighteenth century. He recognized the existence in between the state and the family of a host of "corporations and colleges, estates and communities," and he studied carefully "what profits or inconveniences ensue thereof unto the commonwealth." Some were created by the people themselves and were essentially fellowships of colleagues who agreed to abide by certain common rules, interpreted by certain representative "persons"; they enjoyed the tacit or explicit approval of the sovereign, as long as they treated together "only the things to them common," and did not try to subject non-members to their rules. Others were collegial bodies instituted by the sovereign, such as his parliaments or the estates of the realm; these, too, acquired a life of their own; but they were authorized not only to make rules for themselves but also to exercise authority over his subjects.

In this scheme of things, a municipality obviously belonged more to the latter category: it was authorized or permitted by the sovereign to exercise authority over those of his subjects who came within the area of its jurisdiction; and if it exceeded its powers its leaders could be chastened or its privileges withdrawn.

In a "popular state," absolute freedom would be left to intermediary bodies; in a "tyranny," they would be suppressed. Between these two, however, the "just monarchy" would pursue a middle course. "Monarchies," wrote Bodin, "became corrupted when little by little the privileges of bodies and cities are taken away, and when, instead of limiting themselves to a general supervision, which is alone worthy of a sovereign, princes want to rule everything themselves without any intermediary."

Montesquieu, in his *Spirit of the Laws* (1749) said much the same: "It is dependent and subordinate intermediary authorities that form the essence of Monarchy, that is to say, of a government in which one man rules according to fundamental laws. . . . The fundamental laws necessarily presuppose some middle channels through which power flows. . . . If, in a monarchy, you abolish the prerogatives of the lords, the clergy, the gentry and the cities, you will soon have a Popular State or else a Despotism."

They were thus recognizing to the municipalities and other local bodies a certain constitutional status in the state, with an established role as one of the forces that moderate the power of the sovereign, while at the same time enjoying some delegated sovereign power. On the other hand, the state was not based on them, nor were they democratically composed of all their inhabitants. Intermediary bodies risked becoming little more than privileged hereditary, venal, or corporative oligarchies that had survived from an earlier age. Of all such privileged bodies, urban municipalities came to be regarded as being on the whole the least influential, especially after the establishment of the King's peace contributed to economic development outside their walls and to the rising influence of such rural intermediary bodies as the county magistracy in England and the provincial estates and parliaments of France.

Municipal corporations, however, remained respectable relics, whose records became objects of study worthy of some of the leading antiquaries of the age, from Thomas Madox, historiographer royal of England, with his *Firma Burgi* (1722), to Brequigny of the French Academy of Inscriptions, with his article on Communes in Diderot's *Encyclopedia* (1753).

Intermediary bodies, moreover, became so much a part of the thinking of educated Europeans, that they found them everywhere. Catherine the Great recognized the gentry as an essential part of the Russian constitution and organized them formally by province and by district. Charles Metcalfe, when East India Company resident at the court of the great mughal at Delhi, was lost in admiration of the village communities, which "had preserved the people of that region through all revolutions and changes and were conducive to their enjoyment of a high degree of freedom and independence," to the point where he proposed to make revenue settlements with them as intermediaries rather than to disturb their constitutions by dealing directly with individual landholders.[1]

constituent bodies

An alternative approach was offered by Johannes Althusius (Johann Althusen). Nassau and East Friesland, where he taught Roman Law at Herborn and served as syndic at Emden, stood in much the same relationship to the United Provinces of the Low Countries as did Calvin's Geneva to the Swiss Confederation. Here was living evidence for his theories. He was moreover, a Calvinist, that is to say, the partisan of a presbyterian form of church organization in which every congregation managed its own affairs through elective officers, except insofar as it federated with other congregations and delegated responsibility upwards to a hierarchy of synods in which it was represented.

His *Politics Logically Analyzed* (1603) went through five editions in Latin in fifteen years, finding a market in the Netherlands and Lower Germany before the Thirty Years' War, and then undergoing a remarkable resurrection after the creation of a federated Germany in the late nineteenth century.

Although he took full account of Bodin's views, he departed from them at crucial points, partly because they did not harmonize with the facts of Low Dutch political

---

[1] Sir C. T. Metcalfe, acting governor general, minute, November 7, 1830, in Select Committee *Report* 3:331 in House of Commons *Sessional Papers*, 1832, 11:600.

life, but no less because of his passion for logical method.

Starting from the premise that it was the nature of men to live together in groups, all of which had their common property, services, and rules, he proceeded to classify these groups in an almost pyramidal manner. Some he classed as private, like the natural grouping of spouses and kinfolk in families and the civil grouping of colleagues in gilds. Others he classed as public because they were composed not of individuals directly but of all the groups that lived on a certain territory. Here he gave first attention to the city or city-state (*civitas*) as a grouping together of all the private groups—families and gilds—that happened to live on its territory, as well as sometimes of dependent rural communities. Finally he reached the realm (*regnum*) as the supreme and all-inclusive group of groups (*consociatio consociationum*) of which the corporate members were other public groups —the greater cities or city-states directly and the lesser cities indirectly through the provinces of which they were members. It followed, moreover, from his premises that in the city the municipal corporation consisted of the whole body of private member groups rather than being limited to a select municipal council, just as, in the realm, supreme power rested collectively in the whole body of its public member groups rather than with a personal sovereign.

Here was the classical expression of a minority view that was to find echo in later centuries, whenever efforts were made to treat local bodies as quasi-sovereign units of self-government or as constituent elements from which higher levels of authority were derived. Important, however, as was this piece of Low Country and Calvinist logic, it was the alternative conception of the subordinate "intermediary body" that predominated in Anglo-French thought and practice for nearly two hundred years.

It was to the dominant tradition that John Milton gave a republican twist when he closed his career of public service in 1660 with the declaration that secular freedom "consists in the civil rights and advancements of every person according to his merit . . . which in my opinion may be best and soonest obtained if every countie in the land were made a kind of subordinate Commonaltie or Commonwealth . . . so it be not supreme but subordinate to the general power and union of the whole Republic. In which . . . we shall also far exceed the United Provinces, by having, not as they . . . many Sovranties united in one Commonwealth, but many Commonwealths under one united and entrusted Sovrantie."

2

the governmental subdivision

the age of enlightenment, reason, and utility

during the two hundred years from Bodin to Montes-quieu, the state was conceived less and less as a framework in which intermediary groups could live their own lives, and more and more as an aggregate of individuals. Beginning with Hobbes, and moving on through Hume to Kant, what mattered was the relationship between sovereign and subject, state and individual. Intermediary bodies might, or might not, be useful; but they had less and less life of their own. In the name of reason or utility, their historic privileges could be called in question. With revolutionary radicalism, they could be destroyed. With mathematical precision, they could be reorganized from top to bottom. Such philosophical dif-

ferences as emerged between rationalists and utilitarians
were of little practical effect in regard to local bodies,
except insofar as rationalism became more destructive of
the old and utilitarianism more constructive of the new.

A typical early flight of the mathematical fancy was that
of David Hume in his *Essays Moral and Political* (1741).
His "idea of a perfect commonwealth" was to have one
hundred counties, each divided into one hundred parishes; the whole would then be ruled by one hundred
senators drawn one from each county, and each of these
by ten county magistrates drawn one from each ten
parishes. Catherine the Great actually restructured
Russia arithmetically, with ten districts to a province
(1775).

Rousseau (1762) and Kant in his old age (1793, 1797),
with their new stress on the equal natural rights of every
human person, saw no reason for any group of any kind
between the free citizen and the free state. Kant even
made a point of stressing that the citizens of a state
based on reason were *"citoyens,* i.e., *staatsbuerger,* not
stadtbuerger, i.e., *bourgeois,"* and that such a state was
free to disendow perpetual foundations and corporations
by general legislation. In this he was but echoing Diderot's *Encyclopedia,* where Turgot has written in a fa-
mous article on Foundations: "Particular bodies do not
exist by or for themselves: they have been formed for the
benefit of society and they ought to cease to exist the
moment they cease to be useful" (1757).

According to the contemporary mechanistic way of
looking at human nature, as it had evolved from Hobbes
to Helvetius, the distinction between the general interest,
on the one hand, and, on the other, the special interests
pursued by individuals had to be taken as the starting
point for constructing a new institutional environment
capable of making the public and the private interest
equally attractive. In jurisprudence this involved a conception of the state as the formulator of general laws
rather than as the grantor or upholder of special privileges. In social psychology it invited the state to act as

the civic educator of the people. In economics it meant aversion to special interests that stood in the way of the expansion of the wealth of nations. In political philosophy it might mean ultimately that government must emanate from the generality of the governed by way of election, instead of being the property of the hereditarily privileged. In local administration it was to mean, among other reforms, the conscious creation of governmental subdivisions so organized that they might serve as links between the general interest of the state and the private interests of property-owners and other inhabitants.

It was on bases such as these that a modern theory of Local Government, as distinct from a historic cult of intermediary bodies, was elaborated by French utilitarians by 1775 and by British utilitarians from about 1819.

With their new way of thinking came a new vocabulary. Before long, nothing more was heard of intermediary bodies. The talk was now of the state and its territorial subdivisions; and by the second generation it was in terms of Central and Local Government, central and local authorities, superior and subordinate administrative bodies, *pouvoir central et pouvoirs locaux, centralisation et décentralisation.*

utilitarianism: the Turgot pattern

When Turgot became controller-general and Condorcet and DuPont de Nemours became his inspectors-general at the beginning of Louis XV's reign (1774–76), local bodies became one of the key questions to which they gave their attention. Local administration was considered by them, not in isolation, but as part of the whole problem of radically reforming the state, and giving it a constitution in which the general interest and equality before the law, and especially before the tax law, would triumph over the special interests and privileges of the nobles and clergy, the municipalities, and the gilds. This could not all be done at once. Phasing therefore became all-important. Turgot regarded local administrative reform as a priority phase in his total plan of financial reform and wanted to let people get used to reform at the local level before he carried it up to higher levels. This strategy left intact for the time being the legislative, organizing, and budgeting power of the crown, and claimed to be purely administrative.

Turgot's plan for the reform of local administration was put into writing by DuPont in 1775. It indicated clearly the spirit in which it was composed. Instead of "going back into what our ancestors did in the age of ignorance and barbarity," a ruler, it said, did not need to be prodigiously learned. All he needed was to know men's rights and interests; these were few; and the science that covered them had a high degree of certainty. The rights of men in society were founded not on their history but on their nature. At every level, it would be clear that there was a common good towards which men could combine their force and their resources, serving their own and the general interest at the same time. The crown also would be strengthened by no longer doing—and obtaining un-popularity by doing—what the people could do for themselves.

The full plan envisaged a pyramid consisting of what were called "four levels of municipality." At the base, the whole kingdom would be subdivided into *municipalités de village.* Some thirty of these within a radius of less than fifteen kilometers—permitting a one-day round-trip—would make up a *municipalité d'élection.* Some thirty of these again within a longer radius—the arithmetic was not quite clear—would later form a *municipalité de province.* Lastly, some thirty of these in turn would eventually constitute the *grande municipalité générale du royaume.*

The bottommost "municipality" would be elected by all who had property in the village because one of its func-tions would be to apportion the taxes among them. It would therefore have every inducement to establish a village land-register or cadaster. In order to increase the ability of its land to pay taxes it would be empowered to undertake such local public works as road improvements, which would lessen the wear-and-tear on draft animals, and also to relieve its poorer families, as for example by employing them on these public works. It would also elect a deputy to the next higher level, which would similarly apportion taxes according to resources, undertake public works, and relieve its villages in the event of local disaster. Similarly with the next, up to the highest.

The responsibility of the proposed local bodies for apportioning taxes was an indication that the reform which Turgot had in view was essentially economic and fiscal; for this was to his mind the essence of administration. Putting power in the hands of all who owned land was the counterpart of his long-term plan to have taxes fall on land. He was therefore even ready to consider giving several votes to those who registered extensive property, while permitting registrants of smaller properties to combine to share their vote, hoping that emulation to participate in power and influence would help make men estimate their property generously.

The "municipalities" which he had in view had nothing in common with those of the past. Instead of being based on privilege, they would be based on general legislation. Instead of differing as the result of historic accident, they would be uniform. Instead of being urban, they would be mainly rural. Not least, they were to be a practical form of civic education.

Preoccupation with other problems delayed Turgot's submission to the king of this first or local phase of his total plan of administrative and constitutional reform; and he fell from power before officially publishing, let alone achieving, it. Although not officially promulgated, it was nevertheless privately diffused and proved to be remarkably influential. DuPont's draft was passed around in manuscript, both in France and abroad; he published a summary in the United States in 1782; and from 1787 the entire local reform plan was printed and published in various forms.

application of the Turgot pattern in America and Europe

The influence of this plan radiated widely in both space and time. Either this plan or the spirit that underlay it may have inspired the United States decision in 1784–87 to subdivide the north-west territory geometrically into states, counties, and thirty-six-square-mile self-administering townships, with the lower units represented in the governing organs of the higher ones. In a democratic version it survived into Jefferson's model of tier-on-tier division and subdivision of governmental labor, from nation to township.

It may be presumed also to have influenced not only Sieyes's proposal for a geometrical reconstitution of France into communes, cantons, arrondissements and departements, but also the geographical subdivision that was actually effected in 1790, with the local units all based on representation of property-owners and all aimed at apportionment of taxes, as well as at public works and relief. Under Bonaparte's hegemony, this system spread—although with representation by appointment rather than election—to Western Germany, the Low Countries, Italy, Poland, and, through Spain, to Hispanic America in 1813.

Its essential features became crystallized in the Napoleonic compromise between local agents of central authority and centrally supervised councils representing local interests. By this distinctive combination, the sovereign state made sure, on the one hand, that its laws should be executed and that its view of the general interest should triumph over all lesser interests, as prefects appointed to the departements, sub-prefects to the arrondissements, and maires to the communes, represented the forces that had captured power at the center and supervised the various field services on behalf of all ministries. On the other hand, in order to apportion the taxes needed in the general interest, as well as to levy the additional tax-rate needed locally and to manage the

corporate property of the commune and later the departement, local councils were retained. These were
centrally appointed from among men of local influence
from 1800, like English county benches, and then again
elected, by tax-payers after 1831 in the communes and
1833 in the departements, or by universal manhood suffrage from 1848. However chosen, these were essentially
deliberative and housekeeping bodies subject to supervision by the central agents.

utilitarianism: the Benthamite pattern

The idea that the greatest happiness of the greatest
number could be served by central reorganization of local
administration reached England and its overseas pos-
sessions about 1819—the year when Jeremy Bentham at
the age of seventy became a democrat and a radical and
James Mill went to work at India House.

From now until his death in 1832, Bentham moved on
from the reform of civil and criminal law, lawmaking and
procedure, to that of constitutional law—from the protection of society by government to the constitution of
government itself; and he carried over into this later
phase of his work the same intention of laying down
universally valid principles susceptible of adaptation to
particular circumstances of time and place.

To this new task he also brought a number of principles that he had been expounding as a reformer of judicial administration for the past forty years. One was the
need for a systematic hierarchy of territorial jurisdictions.
Another was that the principal functional difference between the higher and the lower instances was that the
higher established uniform general principles by codification and by hearing appeals, whereas the lower dealt
with particular facts. Another again was that the decision whether to take a particular case in first instance
before the lowest or before a less local tribunal could be
left to the parties concerned: division of labor could be
left to competition or the user's choice. Not least was the

principle that an individual judge was more useful than a bench, provided he had to justify his decisions and to run the risk of their being appealed. All such principles as these were now adapted to non-judicial aspects of administration.

The one important difference that entered in as Bentham turned from penal and civil to constitutional law was that it now seemed to him that the governing authority itself had to be made responsible, and this could be only to the people. Once this democratic principle was accepted, it could be applied equally to what Bentham called "the central and the local government." For it was he who invented the term "the local government." [2]

Bentham's recasting of constitutional, as of penal and civil, law had its negative side. He was appealing to universal reason against the insular traditions of English common lawyers and Whig political philosophers. His conception of local government left no room for the close corporations of the boroughs and the squirearchy of the counties, both irresponsible alike to the central authorities and to the local population. It implied creation by general law rather than privilege and by positive law rather than custom.

Towards 1830, feeling that his end might be near, Bentham summarized his voluminous writings of the last ten years in what he most immodestly entitled a *Constitutional Code for the Use of All Nations and All Governments Professing Liberal Opinions.* In 1843, John Bowring, Bentham's biographer and an authority on comparative fiscal administration, republished this privately printed code, revised and completed from the master's manuscripts, as a volume in his collected *Works.*

Bentham's ideas on local government, as on other aspects of constitutional and administrative law, have

[2] The abstract term "local government" was used by Lord John Russell in the House of Commons, June 5, 1835, in introducing the municipal reform bill, and it figured in the preamble to that bill. The expression "municipal government" was also used by Russell and Sir Robert Peel in parliament in 1835.

thus come down to us in two different printed forms, besides existing also in yet other forms in the abundant manuscripts which he left to future generations. Consequently, there cannot be any one authoritative statement of his doctrine.

His writings contained, nevertheless, certain characteristic approaches. His starting-point was the mathematical subdivision of the territory of the state into all-purpose "districts, subdistricts, bis-subdistricts and tris-subdistricts," each containing some twenty units at the next lower tier.

In each such unit he envisaged an elective "local headman" and an elective local "sublegislature." The sublegislature would give effect to all "government arrangements," insofar as it might be called upon to do so by the supreme legislature. Subject to the authority of the legislature, it would institute and keep on foot such "public works and establishments" as it might think fit, in such fields as prevention of crime and disease, relief of indigence, education, and property-registration; and it would have power to tax or expropriate land for these purposes. The local headman would administer the services thus decided upon, under the direction in every case of the minister within whose field they lay. The local headman and sublegislature would thus be subject to the authority, direction, and inspection of the central legislature and ministers.

One aspect of this local government theory was emphasized at the new University College, London, by John Austin in his *Lectures on Jurisprudence, or the Philosophy of Positive Law,* of which the first volume was published in 1832 as *The Province of Jurisprudence Determined.* His study of legal history under Niebuhr and other German scholars at Bonn had confirmed the impression he had gained from Bentham's attack on the common law, that a distinction had to be made between past ages when law grew and the contemporary age when it was made. In this later age, local bodies were creatures of positive law enacted by sovereign authority. They were

"persons commissioned by the State, to instruct its
subjects . . . , to minister to the relief of calamity . . . ,
to construct or uphold works which require or are
thought to require its attention and interference, e.g.,
roads, canals, aqueducts, sewers, embankments." In
short, they were "subordinate political superiors."

Another aspect of this local government theory was
emphasized by John Stuart Mill in the chapter "on local
representative bodies" in his *Considerations on Representative Government* (1861). He here gave classical
expression to the need for local bodies to be subject to
constant guidance and inspection by the competent
central authorities, not only in the interest of good administration as such, but also in the interest of progress
by way of the education of their members:

The authority which is most conversant with principles
should be supreme over principles, while that which is
most competent in details should have the details left to
it. The principal business of the central authority should
be to give instruction, of the local authority to apply it.
Power may be localized, but knowledge, to be most useful, must be centralized. . . . To every branch of local
administration which affects the general interest there
should be a corresponding central organ. . . . It ought to
keep open a perpetual communication with the localities: informing itself by their experience, and them by
its own; giving advice freely when asked, volunteering
it when seen to be required; compelling publicity and
recordation of proceedings, and enforcing obedience to
every general law which the legislature has laid down
on the subject of local management.

application of the Benthamite pattern in the United Kingdom

The young men who gathered around Bentham found
that they could apply these principles piecemeal by
creating new special-purpose authorities and reforming
the municipalities, without waiting to reform the counties.

The first of several to leave their mark on local government was Edwin Chadwick, who had lived with him as
his literary secretary while preparing for the bar, and in
that capacity had participated in the thinking that went

into the master's Constitutional Code. As commissioner of a royal commission on the poor law, and then first secretary of the permanent general Poor-law Board established in 1834, he was able not only to draft the new poor law but also to administer it according to utilitarian principles. The whole country was subdivided for this specific statutory purpose into "unions"—so called because they were unions of a number of parishes—each of which was essentially a market area; they cut across county lines whenever this seemed expedient; and many were to survive as the "rural districts" of later generations. Their "boards of guardians" were to be elected by local ratepayers. The central board, however, was empowered to issue general orders, laying down the policies that the guardians had to follow and controlling the appointments that they made. The guardians thus became special-purpose agents of a central board, directed and controlled, inspected and audited by its functionaries. They were also compelled by statute to act as local agents of the board at Somerset House for civil registration of births, marriages, and deaths.

Edwin Chadwick next moved on in 1848 to preventive medicine, as commissioner and secretary of the first General Board of Health with power to inspect and report on local application of parliamentary sanitary law, as well as to compel places with abnormally high death rates to set up local boards of health.

Meanwhile, Joseph Parkes, Birmingham solicitor and grandson-in-law of Joseph Priestley, had laid down the principle in a royal commission report in 1835 that municipal corporations ought not continue to be free to spend their corporate income for their members' private benefit; that their corporate property ought to be dedicated to the use of the whole body of householders; and that the common councils entrusted with its management should be elected by all permanently settled ratepayers. In substituting uniformity of government and franchise in the place of variety of ancient practices and privileges, the English municipal reform act of 1835 was as radical as its continental European precursors. It was radical also in subjecting to central administrative control the councils' alienation of corporate property, their making of bylaws, and their districting of their area into electoral wards, thus limiting the self-government of 178 municipalities—all except the one biggest (the City of London), the 67 smallest, and the burghs of Scotland. Except for the statutory obligation to have a Watch Committee, parliament did not impose on them mandatory duties, preferring to place these on elective special-purpose boards set up under general poor-relief, health, and, later, education statutes.

In accordance with the heavy Benthamite and Austinian emphasis on the supremacy of central over local government, the law-courts now extended the doctrine of *ultra vires* so as to limit the activity of all local bodies created by positive legislation. In the case of the new statutory special-purpose authorities this was natural, for they differed from the 1800 authorities created during the previous 150 years only in that they derived their authority from general rather than local acts of parliament. What was less foreseen was that the doctrine of *ultra vires* would be applied also to the reformed boroughs, since they, too, were the children of positive legislation. They were thus prevented from developing into true general-purpose authorities, and instead were made dependent on continual recourse to local acts of parliament whenever they might wish to define or extend their powers. Paradoxically, the principle of central responsibility for local government, as applied by the law-courts, thus became the enemy of the equally Benthamite principles of administrative omnicompetence and of general instead of special legislation.

application of Benthamite patterns in India

In India, selected utilitarian concepts of local administration were systematically applied in two phases, the first with emphasis on responsibility upwards and the

second on responsibility downwards, with an interval of a
generation between the two phases. The earlier phase
was inspired mainly by Bentham's pre-1819 writings and
the latter by the writings of the concluding phase when
he had discovered local government and democracy.

It was while James Mill was "examiner" at India House
(1819–36) that the hierarchy of field administrators was
perfected. He was open to the experience of men like
Munro of Madras, who had already chosen to reform and
bureaucratize the traditional Mughal revenue administration rather than to copy whig checks and balances and
the English landed gentry; and in Elphinstone as governor of Bombay and Bentinck as governor-general, the link
with the utilitarians was direct and personal. In accordance with the principles of omnicompetence and individual responsibility, the functions of collector and
magistrate were to remain concentrated in the district
officer, each of whom was to be in charge of a population
of some 100,000. Over him was set a new creation, the
divisional commissioner, each to inspect in person the
administrative and magisterial work of some ten district
officers, according to the distinction between inspection
from above and administration below, and in order to
ensure that the vast powers vested in district officers
should be responsibly and not arbitrarily exercised.
Through the agency of the district officers, revenue was
to be systematically assessed at two-thirds or one-half of
the economic rent on land, and collected from the cultivators without the intervention of any tax-farming individual. In the south-east this already meant direct relations between the administration and the individual
cultivator. In the north, however, it could mean utilization
of the village community, at least as a collective reve-
nue-farmer in return for a 10 percent commission, and in
some localities as a "co-sharing" collective occupier and
joint cultivator. Village elders, according to the principles
of omnicompetence and responsibility, were also allowed
to continue to settle disputes locally in their panchayats
according to custom or equity in the first instance, sub-

ject to the risk of being competed out of business by the
alternative of access to a less local tribunal and a more
impersonal law and the possibility of appeal to a higher
instance. Thus was preserved and remodeled a system
that methodically combined authoritarian bureaucratic
administration from the top down, with the possibility of
traditional local self-administration at the level of the
cultivators in their villages.

The second wave of utilitarian reform of local administration came in the generation following the mutiny of
1857 and John Stuart Mill's retirement from India House
the next year. Provided the center kept control, the more
liberal reformers now became willing to see actual administration devolved not only on field agents of central
authority but also on representative local bodies. Charles
Trevelyan, for example, could tell a parliamentary committee in 1873 that the Indian Civil Service hierarchy,
which he had helped to build, was a scaffolding that
would lose its importance as an Indian constitution was
completed. In his thinking, this required the building up
of a pyramid of representative councils, from village to
province. These, he said, "would be a school of self-
government for the whole of India, the largest step yet
taken towards teaching its 200,000,000 of people to
govern themselves, which is the end and object of our
connection with that country."

In this same spirit, Gladstone's governor-general-in-
council tried to achieve economy by decentralizing responsibility into the hands of local Indian revenue-payers,
climaxing this policy with a statement of principle intended more for the Indian Civil Service than for Indians:

It is not primarily with a view to improvement in administration that this measure is put forward and supported. It is chiefly desirable as an instrument of political
and popular education. His Excellency in Council has
himself no doubt that, in course of time, as local knowledge and local interest are brought to bear more freely
on local administration, improved efficiency will in fact
follow. But at starting there will doubtless be many failures, calculated to discourage exaggerated hopes, and

even in some cases to cast apparent discredit on the practice of self-government itself. If, however, the officers of Government set themselves, as the Governor General in Council believes they will, to foster sedulously the small beginnings of independent political life; if they accept loyally as their own the policy of the Government; and if they come to realize that the system really opens to them a fairer field for the exercise of administrative tact and directive energy than the more autocratic system which it supersedes, then it may be hoped that the period of failures will be short, and that real and substantial progress will have soon become manifest.[3]

To a radical believer in national self-government, such as Wilfred Blunt, this liberal invitation to civil servants to become civic educators seemed merely a poor first step. Within the establishment, however, it precipitated bitter debate on whether the greatest happiness of the greatest number was better served by a representative or a bureaucratic approach, by locally elected councils or centrally appointed civil servants, by the hopeful liberalism of Trevelyan and Ripon or the fearful authoritarianism—or was it paternalism?—of James FitzJames Stephen and Richard Strachey. Nor could it well be otherwise, as long as the established centralized administration was foreign and the proposed local government was local.

approximation to the Benthamite pattern in France

In the many cross-currents of the great French debate between plebiscitary authoritarianism and constitutionalism, the writings of Bentham and J. S. Mill, circulating in French as well as English, played their part.

On the one side, the prefectoral delegates of central authority could be viewed as agents through whose tutelage the intellectual and economic leadership of the capital could radiate progress over the whole country, while the development of administrative justice could

---

[3] Government of India Resolution, May 18, 1882, Lord Ripon governor general, reprinted, United Kingdom House of Commons *Sessional Papers,* 1883, 51:25.

protect citizens against prefectoral misuse or usurpation of power.

On the other side, administrative decentralization by way of local autonomy became an article of faith among liberal constitutionalists, whose desire for a counterpoise to central power was to be embodied after a long struggle in the legislation of 1871 and 1884, establishing standing departemental commissions and making maires elective.

This late nineteenth-century balance between centralization and decentralization was soon, however, to be tilted in the former direction as the central administrative tribunal—the Council of State—extended its jurisdiction to cover the activities of local bodies, and particularly to substitute its judgment for theirs as to the extent to which they might use public authority to create what they considered a public service.

French local government bodies thus came out of the nineteenth century honored and respected but subject to a dual central control—the general administrative control of the prefect to which must be compared the controls exercised by subject-matter specialists in Britain, and the judicial control of an administrative tribunal to which must be compared the controls exercised by law-courts in the common-law countries and particularly in the United States.

It was the emphasis on central guidance that was represented by Dupont-White, the influential barrister at the Court of Cassation and Council of State who translated Mill's *Considerations on Representative Government* and became the principal French theoretician of relations between centralization and decentralization.

American local government law

Although Bentham and his circle were a well-known point of call for American visitors to London, the evidence of the direct influence of his utilitarianism or that of the Mills is less certain in North America than in Britain, India, or even France. This was partly because, as law reformer, Bentham came up against the contemporary American receptivity to his archenemy, the English common law. His principles, however, were in process of being absorbed into England's law of the land, so that, somewhat paradoxically, English jurisprudence became one of the principal channels through which the ideas that he represented penetrated into North American statutory, judicial, and constitutional lawmaking. In general, moreover, and to an extent that is frequently forgotten, many of the same trends were evident in the States and provinces of North America as east of the ocean.

Thus was created the restrictive American mid-nineteenth-century legal attitude towards Local Government: that administrative responsibility should be delegated by the States to artificial State-created local units, subject to the citizen's right of recourse to State jurisdiction.

On the one hand, just as with England's poor-law unions, States covered themselves with special-purpose statutory or constitutional subdivisions, and particularly with school-districts, whose elective boards would serve as State agents to implement particular public policies. On the other hand, here as in England, law-courts tended to require not only of these "involuntary quasi-corporations" but also of the new city corporations plain grants of authority, and to lean against constructive powers. In the absence of a State administration capable of a continuing and expert supervision of local government, the law-courts played a bigger role than elsewhere; and their interventions were based not only on their interpretation and adaptation of the common law but also on the writing into State constitutions of provisions limiting local taxation and indebtedness, outlawing as extra-municipal such action as the incurring of actionable public indebtedness on behalf of private enterprises, and restricting enactment of special local laws.

On the basic principle of creation by and subordination to the State, there could be no doubt. As was stated by the Supreme Court of Iowa by its chief justice, John F.

Dillon, whose *Law of Municipal Corporations* was to pass through five editions in fifty years:

Municipal corporations owe their origin to, and derive their powers and rights wholly from, the legislature. It breathes into them the breath of life, without which they cannot exist. As it creates, so it may destroy. If it may destroy, it may abridge and control. Unless there is some constitutional limitation on the right, the legislature might by a single act, if we can suppose it capable of so great a folly and so great a wrong, sweep from its existence all of the corporations in the State, and the corporations could not prevent it. . . . They are, so to phrase it, the mere tenants at will of the legislature (1860).

Everywhere in the North Atlantic countries the same principles now applied, whatever the adaptations to differences in institutions, laws, language, and outlook. It was in the spirit of the age to disperse power, to have central government work through local government, to have local government emanate from popular election, to have central controls over local government, and to do all this by general law. Looking for a phrase that would make New England practice intelligible in terms of contemporary European theory, Alexis de Tocqueville wrote of "governmental centralization" being combined with "administrative decentralization" (1835).

3

the self-governing community

the age of romanticism and liberalism

Ideologists of the age of reason and enlightenment had thought in universal terms of human nature as being essentially the same everywhere. They had advocated governmental subdivisions that would cover the entire territory of a state, whether rural or urban. Utilitarians had emphasized the responsibility of these subdivisions upwards to the sovereign authority and technical competence of the center, as well as downwards to an electorate. They had stressed the civic education that would come of this double responsibility. As they came to think in terms of evolution, it was on this practical civic education that they placed most emphasis as the key to progress.

Already, however, some men were thinking in other terms. Nationalists, they were beginning to emphasize the differences that distinguish men and institutions, rather than the likenesses that unite them. Historicists, they were beginning to explain evolution in terms of inevitable forces rather than of rational ends and educational means. Jurists, they were beginning to give custom priority over positive legislation. The community, both local and national, was beginning to be recognized as having a life of its own. "Man has no nature, but only a history," one of the neo-Hegelians is reputed to have said. From a forward-looking ideology of Local Government, the North Atlantic countries were to move towards a backward-looking mythology of "local *self*-government."

This romanticization of the intellectual climate occurred within the wider framework of a liberalism that had more confidence in local and private initiative than in the state. Time and time again, the sovereign state was overthrown, while society and the economy were evolving more rapidly and more continuously than ever before. Government that was at the mercy of social and economic forces more powerful than itself could hardly be regarded as a prime motive force for progress, chief civic educator, or the embodiment of the general interest. Local Government, on the other hand, could share in the freedom accorded to private initiative. The cult of the local community would have to be paid for, however, by a pluralism that treated private forms of corporate enterprise with equal if not greater respect.

It was among Prussian administrators that the first great clash of principle occurred between the dictates of universal reason and the claims of Germanic custom, and by them that a marriage was attempted, which made Prussian municipal reform a thing apart, in some ways more permanently constructive and in others more limited than the French and British reforms of Local Government by which it was preceded and followed. Subsequently it was also mainly in the German universities, and particularly in their chairs of legal philosophy, that new theories of the place of Local Government in social evolution were to be elaborated, and from there that they were to radiate out. Next to these and deeply indebted to them, it was British and American publicists, schooled in the common law, who contributed most to the vitalization of the historic tradition of Local Government during this phase.

the double German heritage

The eighteenth-century cult of "pure practical reason" in government was as prevalent in the German states as in France, Britain, and America. It found one of its most categorical exponents in Immanuel Kant in the university of Koenigsberg. It had dozens of practitioners among high administrators who had been trained in universities where these views prevailed. Above all, it was part of the very spirit of the age.

When the Prussian regular army was destroyed by Bonaparte's nation-in-arms, and the whole organization of the Prussian kingdom was submitted to careful and critical analysis, it was initially in terms of the thinking of the Enlightenment that principles were sought on which Prussia could be rebuilt.

When the Westphalian administrator of the now lost province of Westphalia, Karl baron vom and zum Stein —"the Turgot of Prussia"—retired to his estates at Nassau and set out in a memorandum in June 1807 his views on the way of identifying the Nation with the State, he inevitably thought in terms of the prevailing distinction between the public interest (*gemeinnutz*) and private interests (*eigennuetze*). Instead of people having no scope for their energies and their knowledge except their private and personal satisfaction or the pursuit of metaphysics, he proposed to open to them a wide field of public responsibility in what he called Self Administration (*selbstverwaltung*). For him as for Turgot, this would be a way of harmonizing public and private interests.

This, however, was far from being the only element that entered into the great German national awakening of those years. Among the other factors was a new cult of Germanic history as it could be witnessed in England —the unreformed England of Edmund Burke which had succeeded in standing out against the French Revolution and Empire. This cross current was long to be powerful in Prussia. It provided Stein with a non-French and indeed anti-French argument in favor of a policy that stemmed essentially from principles that had their origin in France. He could base his proposals not only on abstract principle but also on concrete experience, not only on universal reason but also on the genius of a Germanic people.

His fellow-Westphalian and one of the most promising of Prussia's younger provincial administrators, Ludwig Vincke, had studied English internal administration carefully during visits in 1800 and 1807, and now in 1808 set down his impressions in a highly factual hundred-page note that constituted the first comparative study of local administration in modern times. This was widely circulated in manuscript until after Napoleon's defeat and Vincke's return to Westphalia as its administrator, when it was to be published by Niebuhr, the Scots-educated economist-statesman who rewrote Roman history in terms of land-tenure and self-government, as a contribution to the further application of the theories that Stein represented. What astonished Vincke was the absence in England of bureaucracy. Self-administration, as he put it, made administration invisible. British freedom depended more on the method and spirit of administration than on a constitution. Freedom in little things counted for as much as in big ones, and in deeds and practice as much as in words and theories. Above all, unpaid public service according to their means was taken for granted by every one.

Nor was Vincke the only usable exponent of the public spirit of unreformed England. A Genevan who had become a general in the Prussian army had a brother who had become a refugee in England, where the fortune that he spent on anti-French publications won him a knighthood as Sir Francis d'Ivernois. He knew every one, from Pitt to Bentham; and it was with him that Vincke had explored England. A comparison that he published between British, French, and Prussian administrative costs indicated that in 1800 Prussian administration cost two-thirds of that of Britain, although Prussia had only one-third the population and relatively even smaller wealth, as well as a tradition of strict economy. It indicated equally that France in its 100 departements had some 40,000 salaried administrators and judges and 50,000 paid *gardes champêtres,* doing work that was done free of cost by Britain's 4,300 county magistrates and 80,000 unpaid parish officers.

Stein was much impressed by this British example of self-administration as gratuitous public administration by men who had private estates or businesses to manage. In accordance with Turgot's teaching, this new policy of associating the Nation with the State must be initiated at the bottom. In view, however, of the power of the landed interest in East Germany, it was easier to begin with urban municipalities, while waiting for social change to make possible the extension of reform to rural communities. He also noted that many British offices, from the sheriff's to the constable's, as well as service in the militia and on the jury, were obligatory. Stein drew on traditional English practice as an example to be copied, even while drawing on the French enemy for legal models: the universal obligation to serve gratuitously must be coupled with election by the generality of citizens, and both must be brought about by general legislation.

the Prussian ordinance of November 19, 1808

When it came to embodying this policy in law, a draft was prepared by Johann Gottfried Frey, municipal administrator (*polizeidirektor*) of Koenigsberg, which was then serving as temporary capital of the Prussian kingdom. From Kant, Frey had already absorbed the current doctrine, which stressed the power of sovereign authority to make and unmake intermediary bodies on behalf of the people as a whole. In this spirit, Frey took the French legislation of the 1790s as his starting-point, with emphasis on one uniform law for all urban entities, with burgess-ship open and indeed compulsory for all residents who had property, a business, or a profession, and with election of representatives by wards and not by gilds.

To this standard model some older and more traditional principles were added. The deliberative Assembly of elected representatives was to be offset by an indirectly elected Magistracy, with powers of initiative, decision, and administration, with longer terms of office for its members and with a salaried and pensionable full-time Burgomaster. In reminiscence of English "self-government at the king's command," provision was made for burgesses to be "deputized" by the municipality, that is to say, drafted to discharge such community responsibilities as the management of schools and public charities. In respect of their local functions, Prussia's municipalities were to be as free as any other juridical person to manage their properties without tutelage, and even to alienate them when this was necessary and useful, as long as the representative assembly and the magistracy were agreed.

The significance of Prussian municipal reform lay less in what it had in common with the contemporary French and British reforms than in what was peculiar to itself. These distinctive traits proved to have great practical virtue. Based on history, they made the city capable of growth. They inspired a new round of municipal theory on the part of professor-practitioners. They were widely copied in Northern Europe; and they became a standard by which to measure the inadequacies and artificialities of French, British, and American approaches.

One of these virtues was compulsory service by the burgesses. The "Elberfeld system" soon became the classical mid-nineteenth century method of eradicating pauperism. A committee of influential persons would be established by the municipality; subcommittees would be made responsible for the poor within their own neighborhoods, and one of their members for the poor within each block; and it would be their duty to remove the causes of their pauperism by helping them to obtain the work, the schooling, the training, the medical care, and the housing that they needed. From Paris to Warsaw and from Amsterdam to Vienna, this municipally organized individual service of the more fortunate to the less fortunate became a standard Central European approach to problems of individual poverty during the liberal years 1830 to 1914, besides making a deep impression on local "charity organizers" in the United Kingdom and the United States. It was certainly more human as well as more paternalistic than the British utilitarians' preference for coldly impersonal tests that would make the poor prefer independence to dependency.

An even greater virtue was that Prussian cities were also now free to manage their municipal properties as might seem to them best. As real estate developers they were able to face the problems of the unforeseen nineteenth-century industrial and urban revolution by opening up new neighborhoods systematically. They were free to make a profit from real estate transactions and public utility management. They were able to invest in amenities, from park and forests to beer gardens and opera houses.

They were free, moreover, to deal simultaneously with all the varied needs of their inhabitants. Schools, health, and poor-relief were not separate functions entrusted to special-purpose authorities, but interrelated aspects of the life of the city as an organic whole. Nor were they at the mercy of judicial interpretations of a principle of *ultra vires* or of what constituted a public service, for they were free to perform any positive service that they could afford.

The need for external tutelage was lessened by the

internal balance between the indirectly-elected longer-term magistracy and the directly-elected shorter-term assembly. This example of built-in checks was to be cited in the parliamentary debates on English municipal reform, as an argument in favor of having indirectly-elected longer-term aldermen to counterbalance the directly-elected shorter-term councillors.

Not least, the fact that early nineteenth-century Prussian local government reform had to be concentrated in the cities coincided with the dominant role of the bourgeoisie in all aspects of contemporary development, and encouraged the devotees of German nationalism to view their municipal reform as a rebirth of the tradition of medieval municipal liberties, which in the Germanic empire had reached a degree of freedom unrivaled elsewhere in Europe.

Under these circumstances, Prussian cities became the basis of the power of the National Liberal Party—the party of the Vinckes and the Niebuhrs—and a practical training ground for such later theorists of Local Government and parliamentary constitutionalism as Gneist and Preuss, from the revolution of 1848 to that of 1918.

These many virtues were not unaccompanied by certain limitations. As in the French and British systems, these reformed cities became a meeting place or battleground for the antithetical or complementary principles of central bureaucracy and local self-administration. Here it was the bureaucrats who made the reform; and, in the spirit of the Enlightenment, they took care to maintain the sovereignty of the state. Instead, however, of laying a basis for some form of tutelage, they relied on a distinction between two kinds of function. So far as the management of corporate property was involved, they were willing to concede full municipal self-administration. So far, however, as public power was concerned, they insisted that this be exercised by and for the state. Police powers and responsibility for judicial administration within city limits were thus vested not in the municipality but in its burgomaster, viewed for this purpose as an agent of the state, much as was being done also in Napoleonic France; and he was to be selected with central approval and bound to the central authorities by oath. This distinction between centrally-imposed and locally-assumed functions (*beauftragteangelegenheiten* and *selbstverwaltungsangelegenheiten*) was of course to have many counterparts or echoes in other systems of Local Government law. As already noticed, the English municipal reform act was to make municipal police mandatory while making no provision under general law for service activities. Other practices that were to bear even closer resemblance were to include the American judicial differentiation between the governmental and the proprietary functions of local bodies and the line that French jurists were to draw between *actes d'autorité* and *actes de gestion.* In France and the United States, however, this line of demarcation was to be part of the process of defining the jurisdiction of the courts before which a private person might bring a case, whereas in Prussia it established a battleground between the central ministry and the municipal assemblies. This theoretical dichotomy was to prove as hard to define or defend in Prussia as elsewhere, owing to the increasing practical interlocking between police powers and expanding service activities.

This reform, moreover, applied only to urban communities. In the rural communities of eastern Germany, administration and justice remained attached to the hereditary patrimony of their lords.

The advance from local self-administration to parliamentary constitutionalism, desired by Stein as by Turgot, was not yet feasible. Stein might subdivide the kingdom into administrative districts (*regierungsbezirke*) much like French departements; but the time had not yet come when representative councils could be associated with their administration, and they could be made the next step in a pyramid of constitutional progress. Prussia thus became the first modern country in which the principles of self-government and of representation by election were introduced to some extent at the local level while being indefinitely postponed at the center, providing in this respect an example that was to be followed by the Ottoman, the Russian, and the Indian empires.

the local community hallowed by history

Ever since the idea of progress had emerged in the late eighteenth century, it had been axiomatic among economists and historians, from Adam Smith to Guizot, that the medieval bourgeoisie and their municipal privileges were the cause of which modern industry and rationalism were the effect. If, however, one thought in terms of a tradition of self-government rather than of economic and social progress, one might take account of local liberties in general rather than of urban liberties alone, especially since the tradition of local self-administration was still very much alive in rural England and New England, as Vincke and Tocqueville had reported.

Taking this broader and deeper view, a veritable cult of the local community, with Local Government as its organ, emerged soon after 1848.

It was Toulmin Smith in England who first appealed to historic continuity in an overt fight against utilitarian reforms. Fresh from lecturing on the Vikings in New England, he took part in suburban Highgate's measures to protect itself against cholera in 1848, without waiting for central authority to take the initiative, and then built up a practice at the parliamentary bar on behalf of local bodies when private and local legislation was under consideration. A tirade entitled *Government by Commission Illegal and Pernicious* (1849) was quickly followed by others on *Local Self-Government and Centralization* (1851) and *The Parish* (1854), and these by the organization of an Anti-Centralization Union (1854–57).

For the first time the term "local self-government" was let loose on the English language, with the explicit meaning that all outside interference should be excluded —an attitude that ran completely contrary to the newly established policy and practice of Great Britain as of all North Atlantic governments in that age. Here, in the name of freedom and progress, was an attack on the essential elements of the liberal reforms of his day. His faith was in the historic units such as the unreformed borough and the parish, the responsibility of their officers to folkmoots or town meetings, and their exercise of the widest possible powers, preferably under the common law and by prescription from time immemorial. His opposition was to all forms of central interference, whether by acts of parliament establishing special-purpose authorities, or by local acts granting specific powers, or by general acts replacing direct democracy with representative bodies, or by central supervision of local administration.

In South Carolina this new language was immediately taken up by Francis Lieber in his much-reprinted college textbook *On Civil Liberty and Self-Government* (1853). It fitted in with the political science he had introduced into the United States as the study of the relationship between individuals and history-begotten nations as living organic systems. Quoting Toulmin Smith and Niebuhr, in whose household he had once lived, he emphasized the Anglo-American tradition of what he called "articulated liberty" and "institutional self-government," "self-evolving, interguaranteeing and interlimiting," in which much of the administrative branch is left to the people, especially in their counties.[4]

Meanwhile, in Western Germany, George Maurer was collecting material for twelve volumes on the history of local units, from the frontier settlement through the village and manor to the town, which were published between 1854 and 1871. A Palatine protestant jurist, he had administered French codes in a land of German custom, had helped codify the law of the new kingdom of Greece with due respect for the customs preserved by the

[4] The new word "self-government" was traced back by Lieber to Jefferson (1798) in the sense of the power of the States to manage their internal affairs without external interference. In British usage it came to be similarly applied to internally self-governing colonies.

community while under Ottoman rule, and had served as anti-clerical prime minister of Bavaria on the eve of the revolution of 1848. What he now set out to show was why some states progressed while others remained backward and how it was that they progressed. This led him to trace modern liberalism back to urban liberties and then to show that these in turn had their roots in the soil. The rural community thus made its appearance as the cell from which all freedom—political, economic, and religious—had evolved; and the historical approach, which German scholarship had recently applied to the state and the law, was now thoroughly and exhaustively applied to land rights and the local community.

The evolutionary approach to law, which was now commonplace in German universities, was introduced to the English-reading public by Henry Maine's *Ancient Law* in 1861. In this best-seller, as in his lectures in Roman law at Oxford and in jurisprudence at the Inns of Court, he had drawn on descriptions of India, as well as research into Roman and Germanic law, in order to show that the Benthamite-Austinian view of law as the command of the sovereign was valid only in certain circumstances and at certain stages of development. In his search for the origin of property, he made a particular point of showing how recent and how far from universal was the modern Western concept of absolute private ownership. He illustrated his argument by reference to what he believed to be the extreme antiquity and apparent indestructibility of a quite different practice in North Indian village communities, viewed not as neighborhoods of unrelated freeholding individualists, but as brotherhoods of kinsmen who were at the same time societies of co-partners. In its search for origins, this little classic popularized the backward-looking aspects of the concept of social evolution, much as Darwin's *Origin of Species* had done for biological evolution only two years earlier. It won for its author seven years in India as legal member of the Governor General's council. This in turn gave him an opportunity for closer contact with men familiar with

Indian villages and brought him back to Oxford as first
incumbent of a new chair of comparative jurisprudence,
where in 1869 he gave six lectures on *Village-Communities in East and West,* bringing together the results of
Maurer's research in Germany and his own hypotheses.

In North India as in Germany and England, he found
communities carving their arable out of their waste lands,
cultivating their arable according to customary rules interpreted by the community, becoming close corporations
opposed to admitting outsiders to share in their common
fund, and liable to the transformation of community rights
into private property by some one man being made responsible for gathering—and being sometimes permitted
to retain—the royal land-revenue. These similarities
impressed him more than the difference, which also he
noted, between the Anglo-German town meeting of
weapon-bearing males and the Indian usage of having a
headman (*patel*) or representative elders (*panchayat*) to
define custom. It was unfortunate for Maine's later reputation that out of this pioneering and penetrating
analysis of incomplete evidence came not only a knighthood for the author but also the untenable hypothesis
that English, German, and Indian villages and New England towns were all alike descended from the same institutional ancestor, the Aryan village community—a truth
revealed to him by the new science of comparative jurisprudence, just as comparative philology had recently
uncovered a proto-Indo-European mother language.[5]

In North America, after civil war and reconstruction
had lessened the self-government of the States while
increasing opportunities for collective action at the local
level in the southern States, a still predominantly rural
nation soon learned the antiquity and universality of
grass-roots democracy. From Freeman of Oxford it heard

[5] The comparative method seems to have meant something different
then from what it means now. Then it meant a search for similarities
as evidence of common ancestry, rather than a typological construction of alternative models to which phenomena are expected to
correlate.

that it was the latest of the three homes of Teutonic local liberties: Germany, England, and New England. Around Herbert Adams at Johns Hopkins University, who himself wrote on the Germanic origin of New England towns, there gathered graduate students from many States who made rural local institutions, both past and present, into objects of academic research. Above all, as the new rearward look at social evolution was combined with the older vision of human progress, there arose in the United States a faith in an advance that started from local liberties to end the federation of mankind. This optimistic evolutionism, akin to that of Herbert Spencer and Thomas Huxley, found its popularizer in John Fiske of Yale, Harvard, and the Royal Institute of Great Britain. By 1880 he was delighting audiences by tracing back the town meetings of New England to the village assemblies of the early Aryans, making the federalism that began with these local units the key to heaven on earth, and drawing on the history of the English and the French in North America to prove that "local self-government" was stronger and more fit to survive than "bureaucracy." He provided students with the first textbook on American government that began with the township and worked upwards. In an age that combined nationalism with laissez-faire, it became normal to play down the State and play up the municipal corporation. In American jurisprudence, the nadir of the State found its corollary in the zenith of the municipality. Thus Thomas M. Cooley in his *Constitutional Limitations* (1868) declared that "by the customs of our race" municipal organs had a common-law power of legislation, any prohibition on the delegation of State legislative powers to the contrary notwithstanding, as well as being entitled to the same immunities and protection as attend State action, and that the continuance and perpetuity of "the system of local self-government" were the purpose for which all American constitutions were formed.

It was in this climate of opinion that American municipalities tried to fight off State legislative interference by arguing that New England towns had incorporated themselves before ever there were any written State constitutions, that local bodies had been run time out of mind by locally chosen officials, and that local self-government was an inherent or common-law right reserved to themselves by the people. These mythological arguments by legal counsel were reflected in dicta by a number of State judges, beginning with Cooley in a Michigan case in 1871; they may perhaps have helped some courts so to interpret State constitutions as to annul a few pieces of legislation that would have extended State action in fields claimed by municipalities; and the unguarded language used by judges and writers of legal textbooks contributed to an atmosphere in which Local Government was widely revered as part of the unwritten constitution of a republic that was now learning to distrust the States and their positive legislation.

local self-government in the idealist philosophy

For a hundred years Hegel's conception of man's evolution as a dialectic between community, society, and state, haunted the thinking of German legal and social philosophers. It was in terms of this dialectic that Gneist and Lorenz Stein, Gierke and Toennies, Weber and Preuss, idealists and materialists, asked new questions and propounded new answers on the role and value of local institutions in the life and evolution of humanity.

The problem that Rudolf Gneist posed after the revolution and reaction of 1848 was how to prevent revolution and assure law-respecting evolution, or, in Hegelian terms, how to effect a synthesis between state and society. This synthesis he believed for a while he had found in the England which he had visited about 1840, and in which he had observed those social elements without which the introduction into continental Europe of British constitutional conceptions of limited monarchy (1815–30) and parliamentarism (1830–48) had had only limited success.

His *Present-day English Constitutional and Adminis-*
trative Law (1860) had, as its second part, *The Consti-*
tution and Administration of the English Community
Today; or, The System of "Self-Government" in Its Pres-
ent Form. In it he marshaled evidence for his thesis that
local self-government was a prerequisite to national
self-government and that administrative reform in this
sense was, as he used to say, "constitutional reform from
the inside out."

What he vaunted was not English local administration
as a whole, but only part of it, the same part as Vincke
had found so admirable and Stein had held up for imi-
tation half a century earlier: the sheriffs and county
magistrates, grand jurors and petty jurors, parish over-
seers and constables, who were drafted, more or less
willingly, under the common law, for the gratuitous
service of the crown in their counties and parishes. For
the new statutory system of utilitarian local boards as
they had meanwhile evolved in Britain, with their dual
responsibility to electors below them and to central
technical administrators above, he had no use; their
functions were to him mere housekeeping, not self-government; protection of private interests, not assumption
of public duties. His application of the term "self-government" to British local affairs as they were now
evolving was, strictly speaking, as anachronistic as in the
writings of Toulmin Smith, from whom he probably borrowed it. He lamented with him the trends that were
working towards an elective county administration; and,
because he was dealing with a passing rather than an
emerging England, none of his writings on local administration has ever been translated into English. It was
through him that Bismarck's Germany knew England's
tradition of public spirit, but misknew its contemporary
institutions and overstressed the role of autonomous
centrally-appointed local commissions acting through
quasi-judicial procedures. Putting the same reflection
another way, it was through him that Germany learned
those aspects of British local administration that were

related to its own conscious needs and attitudes, and that seemed to it—only half correctly—to be in harmony with the principles of Baron Stein.

Himself a city councillor at Berlin from 1848, as well as a professor of public law at the University of Berlin and a member of the Prussian house of representatives, Gneist gained the reputation of a technician as well as a theorist of Local Government. He advised Bismarck on the Prussian local administration reforms of 1872 and the following years, which provided for representative local landowners to sit on councils in the arrondissements (*kreise*), and to share in tutelary supervision over rural communes and in administrative justice at the local level. Thus would be linked together what he regarded as the British tradition of quasi-judicial "self-government at the king's command" and the European continental need for recourse to administrative justice, as two ways of encouraging the bureaucracy to administer the state in accordance with consent and legality. To him—and it was perhaps his greatest cause for fame and influence in other European continental countries—the state that worked through local bodies was a state that worked also through law. Conversely, the "law-state," as he called it, was a state that could count on citizen participation. The upbuilding of constitutional government meant the articulation of the state. He advised also on the statutory authorization of local taxing powers so that local bodies could set a tax rate on their constituents' properties, businesses, and professions, with which to cover the gap between their corporate income and their total outlay. He helped in the consolidation of the Prussian legal doctrine that the better half of the duty of local office-holders was to carry out the orders of the state, expressed as much through its administrators as through its legislature, and that local notables who participated in this process were honorary state officials. His philosophy was happily summed up by a British liberal writing for the Cobden Club: "Self government means the harnessing of Society to the State, not the disintegration of the State into

joint-stock companies ruled by boards of elected directors. . . . It was the carrying out the will and doing the
work of the State by the local units of society themselves,
and not the carrying out the will and the doing the work
of the local units by means of delegates or representatives named by these units."

More cosmopolitan and less German or Anglo-German
in his approach, more concrete and indeed material in his
view of the functions of modern government, and less
well-known in the English-speaking world, was Lorenz
von Stein. He knew the France of the 1840s even more
intimately than his friend Gneist knew England; and with
this knowledge came a greater concern for the interplay
of forces making for change than for those making for
continuity. He had particularly studied French municipal
organization and had made a name for himself by several
volumes on the capture of state power by social move-
ments in that country. Fleeing from Danish-ruled Slesvig
to a chair of public law at Vienna, he taught administration as a "good European" by the comparative method
that he considered particularly suited to the economic
and social development of the multinational Hapsburg
dominions as well as to the Japanese students who came
to Vienna to know Europe.

As he looked back, Stein recognized the seventeenth
and eighteenth centuries as a phase that preserved the
forms of local liberty while bypassing the historic communities whenever new services had to be administered.
He recognized also that during what he called Europe's
constitution-making phase, from 1789 to 1848, the de-
struction of privilege by the general legislation of the
sovereign state had changed the forms of local organization, establishing a general trend in Europe towards
locally elected deliberative bodies, coupled with varying
measures of local responsibility to central organs for
ensuring the local application of centrally determined
policy. What he maintained, however, was that since 1848
a new phase was emerging in which the competing interests that made up society and the concern for coop-

eration that was the essence of the state were freely combining to meet practical needs—in which he was more interested than some Prussian contemporaries—by developing two forms of "free administration": the one was Local Government while the other was voluntary association.

To Stein both were equally important, and these two parallel patterns of state-regulated social action were reacting on one another. The voluntary association (*verein*), whether a business corporation, a professional body, a cooperative society, a trade union, a fraternal order, or a subscription charity, was a group formed in accordance with the law to serve a common utilitarian purpose through officers elected to represent the bene-ficiaries or patrons. Local Government also, he observed, was evolving in a similar direction, with a tendency to-wards statutory specification of its purposes, service and answerability to its users, voluntary office-holding, and employment of paid agents.

Thus the very innovations that the conservative Gneist deplored at Berlin, the liberal Stein raised to the center of his thinking at Vienna. Both alike, however, postulated Local Government of one kind or another as a principal method by which the interaction between state and so-ciety could facilitate economic and social progress while perhaps lessening the chances of violent upheavals.

With this theory of the simultaneous incorporation of governmental and nongovernmental agencies for the meeting of common needs, Lorenz Stein became also a pioneer of a pragmatic kind of pluralistic approach to local and other organization within the state.

Most influential outside as well as inside Germany was the analysis of corporate action by Otto von Gierke. The problem that he posed as a soldier-professor in Prussia's wars of German unification was how to resolve what he regarded as the contemporary dialectic between au-thority and liberty, unity and diversity, within the broader framework of what seemed to him to be a continuing di-alectic between Latin and Germanic traditions, tending

the one to exacerbate and the other to resolve this con-
flict. Here he saw the historic mission of the now trium-
phant German political genius: the synthesis of the an-
titheses of authoritarian state and libertarian society. This
synthesis he called *genossenschaft,* a word that means
literally "fellowship" in contrast with "lordship" (*herrsch-
aft*), but in twentieth-century English might perhaps be
rendered as "group life."

Treating as German many phenomena that were
equally English or French, he consecrated five thousand
pages of print and a lifetime of teaching to the rehabili-
tation of the reality of group life, particularly in the four
massive volumes of his *German Law of Group Life,* ex-
tracts from two volumes of which have been translated
into English.

Its second volume was devoted in 1873 to the *History of
the German Idea of Corporate Life* (koerperschaft, which
he distinguished from incorporated bodies). Following in
Maurer's footsteps he once again worked over the history
of German local institutions, not however this time to see
in them the source of freedom in general, but to find them
the embodiment of the concept of group freedom, with
which alone he was concerned. Whereas private law
since the time of the Romans had turned on the rights
inherent in individuals, public law should now hinge on
the rights of groups. For the emergence of this concept, a
beginning was found in the local institutions which in the
Germanic lands had evolved of their own accord into
communities with their common chests and collective
status, and had sought to ensure their communal liberty
by banding together in wider communions. This natural
law under which organized local groups lived a continuing life of their own had come up against opposition
on the part of rulers and incomprehension on that of
officials trained in the Roman law; for this had no tradition of rights immanent in a group, but held instead that
rights other than those of physical persons derived from
external authority which, by an act of its will, incorporated the group as an artificial person or endorsed the

establishment of a foundation by the will of a physical person outside the beneficiary group. Such liberty as local communities had enjoyed since the reception of Roman law was therefore only the little allowed to them by positive law and, even under reforms such as Baron Stein's, was largely for the purpose of managing their property.

With the rise of nineteenth-century nationalism Gierke envisaged the state itself as a community of citizens rather than the property of a ruler. The possibility had thus been opened up of a synthesis between group freedom and state authority—a group freedom that was now transcendental rather than either immanent in the group (as under the German law of the middle ages) or derived by grant from an external authority (as under Roman law). Under this new freedom, the local community, with rights of action as wide as those of a physical person, with its local affairs broadly interpreted, and with all the powers needed to manage them, might also recover a civic spirit, the fellowship of a rich cultural life, and a real sense of belonging.

Gierke's conception of autonomous group life, although inspired by the local community of the past, was directed towards the business corporation of the future. It was in this sense in particular that he became a pluralist. He thought of business corporations and other voluntary bodies, as well as organized local communities, being set free from arbitrary restraints, to develop in accordance with generally accepted and broadly stated standards; it was in the recognition by the German civil code of the real life of these bodies that Gierke became most interested, leaving to his colleague Gneist the detailed study of Local Government and its place in the general system of public law, and to their student Hugo Preuss the task of building local liberties into the written constitutional law of the future Weimar republic.

While Toulmin Smith had thought of freedom growing upwards from its local roots, Gneist thought of it flowing down from the highest state authority; and both views were to find echoes in many countries. To Gierke both represented phases in development that were now synthesized or transcended.

municipal socialism: British pattern

The generation around 1900 lived in what was in many ways a golden age of municipal and local government. Local government units financed themselves. They rendered to their inhabitants more services than were provided by the national government. Local captains of industry and commerce were proud to hold municipal office. Liberal and socialist reformers fought for the extension of municipal powers and the improvement of municipal organization.

"It is to decentralization," wrote Maurice Hauriou in France, "and to the fact that it has associated the entire population with the work of government, that we owe the immense public works effected in the past fifty years: the construction of a network of local roads, the restoration of practically all the churches and of all the clergyhouses of the rural communes, the building of school-houses, and, in the cities, the innumerable highway engineering works, the boulevards, the broad streets, and the parks and gardens, which have transformed them" (1892).

"In times of peace, indeed," wrote Sidney Webb in England, "local government has become, in the advanced countries, in the aggregate, actually more extensive than the central or national government; apart from the payment of interest on all debts, it often spends more money and has many more officials in its employment; it usually carries on more enterprises and conducts more services for the common good. It even enacts, in its by-laws and regulations, a greater volume of laws that we have to obey than the national legislature" (1915).

In the presence of so stupendous a phenomenon, controversy and study were to be expected. These found one of their principal focuses at London, particularly among the thinkers and writers clustered around Sidney and Beatrice Webb, he a solicitor turned leader of the Progressives on the new London County Council and she the leading researcher into nonprofit popular organizations.

The Webbs' own work was enormous. In four volumes they studied the history of the parish and county, the manor and borough, and the newer statutory authorities for special purposes, from the revolution of 1688 to the reform of 1835, largely providing the facts that confirmed Gneist's views of that vanished epoch, besides bringing down to their own day, in another ten volumes, the history of poor-relief, health services, highways, prisons, liquor-licensing, and grants-in-aid. At the London School of Economics and Political Science they brought in as lecturers on Local Government such men as Laurence Gomme, then on his way to becoming clerk to the London County Council, and Percy Ashley, whose lectures became an international textbook, besides others who shared more closely their Fabian socialism, from Clement Attlee and Lees-Smith to William Robson, as well as promoting student research and publication on local government in other parts of the empire from Scotland to India and on such specific topics as local tax-rates, central-local financing, and local legislation.

They had the consciousness of doing something new and important. As Gomme said with some exaggeration, "The principles of government by authorities not dependent upon parliament and the crown, but which are, nevertheless, entrusted by parliament and the crown with certain functions of government, . . . have never been inquired into and determined up to the present time. . . . No great authority, like Austin, or Bentham, or Mill, has thought fit to determine the principles of local government as distinct from the principles of government in general."

What were some of the principles of Local Government on which English practitioner-theorists agreed?

Firstly, from the German legal philosophies, the Webbs accepted the group as a basic fact of human life, while systematically underestimating the utilitarian reforms. As part of their revolt against laissez-faire competition, their research was focused on three forms of nonprofit group life, all enterprising without being entrepreneurial: they reached the "consumers' compulsory territorial association" known as Local Government, to which most of their work from 1897 was devoted, by way of the "consumers' and producers' voluntary organizations" known as cooperatives and trade unions.

Secondly, they identified the self-governing local group as a product of history. Gomme, as an antiquary and folklorist as well as an administrator, defined Local Government "properly-so-called" as something that had developed from the common interests of historic communities—meaning in England the county, the borough, and the parish—and that contained "more of the natural history of men than any other parts of modern civilization," while Sidney Webb wrote of Local Government being "as old as the hills." So far from local government units being subdivisions of the state for purposes of administrative decentralization and civic education, as in utilitarian theory, they were, said Gomme, "traceable to deeper instincts in our life than legislative experiments"; and "local government in its true form is that part of the whole government of the country which is not surrendered by localities to the state, but has ever remained in the hands of the community of persons who originated it."

Thirdly, certain units were of primordial importance. Said Gomme: "The area formed by the common interests of a community dating for centuries back in the past is the true locality within which common benefit from new functions of local government will best operate." The Webbs agree that the restoration of democratic county administration since 1888 ought to be followed by the merger of statutory special purpose authorities into the historic units of government, wherever these still commanded the people's interest.

Fourthly, the dimensions and interrelationships of local

government organization should develop to meet new needs. Historic units should be adapted to changes in the community pattern, and the rise of new communities recognized. The area covered by a service should be as large as was needed for the service as a whole and for recruiting persons big enough to run it. The larger unit might well take over from the smaller if it was the smallest that could really benefit the people. Usually this would mean working through the county and county borough, rather than any lower tier of authority. Sometimes it might mean nationalization of hitherto local services, as had happened with prisons and was going to happen with the employment service, income security, hospitals, and electric power. If intermediate regions were needed for specific services, the historic general-purpose units should be grouped together on whatever scales might be most convenient, but with responsibility always running through the elective bodies in the principal units. H. G. Wells came out of science fiction to tell the Fabian Society that this adaptation of scale to technology ought to be the supreme principle, even if it led, for the sake of simplicity and individual convenience, to forgetting group life and historic units: human life was already so delocalized that one might as well adopt watersheds as the only scientific administrative areas, and abolish most of the lesser units.

Fifthly, Local Government thus constituted and freed from judicial, statutory, and sub-legislative restraints, should enjoy as large a measure of freedom and dignity as possible. Even as it was, initiative and enterprise came as often from local as from central government. The principal historic units ought to be recognized as being true general-purpose authorities, exempt from the *ultra vires* doctrine applied to them by the law courts since the mid-nineteenth century, and therefore freed from the need to spend millions every year on private-bill legislation. In particular, they should be free to furnish their public with any service that they could afford, by way of self-financing "municipal socialism" and the provision of

all manner of free educational, cultural, and health facilities. The new invention of grants-in-aid could con-
tribute to municipal liberty insofar as they were given on
a "block" instead of a "specific" basis.

municipal reform: American pattern

Simultaneously the United States awoke to the fact that
it was on its way to becoming an urban society with a
municipal problem but no urban municipal tradition. It
had barely discovered the historic affinity of the New
England town to the English and Germanic village community, when it learned the inadequacy of rural institutions in a world that was being transformed by capitalism
and technology.

Americans of civic conscience were particularly
shocked by the contrast between the ethics of government in their new cities and that which they believed to
be normal in those of the old world of Europe. It was the
work of a Briton, James Bryce's *American Commonwealth,* which in 1888 provided them with the most detailed and best authenticated evidence "that the government of cities is the one conspicuous failure of the
United States." It was to Britain and continental Europe
that Albert Shaw from Johns Hopkins looked, to give his
fellow countrymen in 1894 a picture in eight hundred
pages of what a modern city could be like—Paris, with a
plan that had made it a city beautiful as well as en-
hancing property values; Germany, where he found no
limits whatever to municipal functions, and it was the
business of the municipality to promote in every feasible
way its own welfare and that of its citizens; and Britain,
with Sidney Webb's progressives building up the new
London County Council and with municipal trading being
extended everywhere.

Americans were no less shocked by the contrast between their municipal practice and their own constitutional principles. When it came to institutionalizing municipal reform, it was to the traditions of their public law

that they were inclined to look. A jurist such as Frank J. Goodnow found that the study of the idealist dialectic helped him towards distinguishing between politics and administration, ideas and mechanics. He found that the study of European municipal institutions helped him analyze American needs and select some approaches rather than others from the American heritage; basically, however, he would not attempt to import foreign institutions. The problem was felt to be too essentially American: it was the fundamental American principles of republican democracy that were challenged, and in them an answer had to be found. In this country at that date, Local Government was not merely one of the instruments of State administration: it *was* State administration, and without it there could then be no other. It had to be made to work, if America was to be true to its traditions and American government was to retain its distinctive national character.

If interest-ridden city administration reflected interest-ridden State legislation, the principle of self-government could best be saved by applying it more systematically to the cities. By "municipal home rule," these must be allowed to organize themselves. They must be freed from State legislative interference. They must be given the powers and resources needed for their policing and the assuring of public and social services. Their rights, rather than their limitations, must be enshrined into State constitutions, so that State judges might have positive ground for liberal rather than restrictive interpretation of municipal powers. If checks on power were needed, the State as then constituted would be less able here than in Europe to supply a continuing supervision from above; in its place, local checks could be built in, perhaps by a Federal type of interplay of mutually independent executive and legislative, perhaps by a reserve of direct local democracy in the forms of the initiative, referendum, and recall, but mainly by clarifying the responsibility of local executive and "legislature" to the local electorate. At the same time the responsibility of

salaried appointive officials to unofficial outside patrons
could be lessened by municipal civil service systems. The
freeing of the cities for self-government might even reduce the States to being little more than outgrown intermediaries.

The municipal reform movement of the 1890s, with its
publications, its clubs, its league, and its conferences,
culminated in 1900 in a comprehensive program in which
all these elements came together. Here was a model
susceptible of adaptation to State constitutional and
statute law and to city home-rule charters. Here was the
consecration of a new and distinctively American tradition. Municipal Science became a regular university
course, with well-ordered textbooks, comparative in
approach.

What was not emphasized by the constitutionalist
American municipal reformers of this generation was that
most American cities did not come as near as German
cities to being communities that met a wide range of
common needs through a single official organ, but instead that they exemplified Stein's theory of voluntary
corporate action being as effective as public, and
Gierke's of business corporations having as free a group
life as any municipality. The American municipality,
however well they reformed it, was but one organization
in a pluralist society of competing organizations.

In the United States, as a consequence, there arose a
considerable body of theory to the effect that the gov-
ernance of an American city was shared or divided between privileged business and the municipal government,
so that the latter, even if reformed, must necessarily
count for less than was the fact in Germany or the hope
in Britain. Municipal home rule might change the formal
structure, but could not add to the powers of a local
government body. The most it could do was to make the
municipality strong enough to hold its own and serve the
general interest of its citizens when bargaining with
public works contractors and public utility concession-
aires. The chorus of well-informed but critical and not

wholly optimistic publicists was typified on the eve of
World War I by Lincoln Steffen's scholarly reporting,
Frederic Howe's frequent and numerous comparisons
with Europe, Tom Johnson's autobiography, and Delos
Wilcox's campaign for public ownership of public utili-
ties.

premonitions

The view that history belonged to Local Government
was not shared by all legal and social theorists at the turn
of the century in Germany any more than in the United
States. Some such as Toennies were to pose such so-
ciological questions as what exactly was a local community. Some such as Weber were to ask whether there
was any rational alternative to professionalism, bureaucracy, and technocracy.

Nonlegal, and therefore indirectly rather than directly
related to Local Government, was Ferdinand Toennies
who in 1887 completed the evolution from Hegelian
philosophy to sociology, with his much-published *Community and Society: A Treatment of Communism and
Socialism as Empirical Culture Patterns.* Under the influence of contemporary imaginings about the anatomy
and physiology of the social organism, he carried a step
further the historical outlook of Maine, Gneist, and Gierke
on the community (*gemeinschaft*), on the one hand,
and, on the other, the rationalism of Lorenz Stein towards
civil society (*gesellschaft*), distinguishing sharply between the origin and evolution of the organic Community
and the purposive creation of a mechanically contrived
State-and-Society. Stretching his terms, he saw on the one
side the Community, whether it were the family, the clan,
the pioneer settlement, the village, the medieval commune, or even the symbiosis of a market town with its
country-side, and, on the other, the State enforcing con-
tractual obligations in protection of individual liberty and
property, the big city in which the location of work-place
and residence were almost accidental, elective represen-

tative bodies, and competition and coercion. It was not
that he preferred the one to the other, but that he provided
a new thought-pattern or fantasy-form by his summing up
of man's institutional history as evolution from an original
familial communism through big-city individualism to
state and international socialism; and from this were to
be derived new tools of analysis, turning particularly on
the distinction, of as much importance to Local Government as to anthropology, between man's more inti-
mate institutional environment and the wider world that
he creates. If the "natural community," as distinct from
the organized local body, has a prophet, he is Toennies.
In his old age, he was to find a new renown among
German nazis preaching community of race and American
rural sociologists faced with open-country neighborhoods
that lacked formal organization.

Last of the German post-Hegelian line of philosophers
of legal history and the most learnedly comparative in his
overview of world legal systems in their cultural contexts,
although the least in his contribution to thinking about
Local Government, was Max Weber (*Economics and
Society,* 1925). His evocation of western medieval municipal liberties, unlike that of many of his predecessors,
stopped short with their unique contribution to the creation of the modern state. His cult of bureaucratic government reduced local bodies to "externally instituted territorial groups," the heads of whose administration might
be appointed equally well from within or from without,
and in which elective officials constituted a hangover of
dilettantism that had become marginal in a world of
expertise. Though using the terminology of Stein and
Gierke as well as Toennies, he moved beyond them to
imply that Local Government as self-government belonged
to history.

4

a local service agency

the problems of local administration in the twentieth century are so multifaceted and so interlocking that no responsible thinker would dare claim that Local Government as such offers either a simple means or the best means of finding solutions. So many professions now participate in local administration that it is the thinking of all and each of them that has its impact and has to be considered, and no longer primarily that of men of law. It is perhaps for these reasons that one can no longer identify any one clear current of legal or social philosophy that today is demonstrably molding the law and structure of Local Government. Moreover, as in the middle ages, much theory is merely implicit in the assumptions or presuppositions that underlie collective behavior.

The various contemporary attitudes or approaches would seem, however, to fall into a few distinguishable types. In the technologically developed countries of the North Atlantic, one approach to local administration has arisen from a pragmatic recognition of the need for centrally-promoted but locally-executed services, while another has explored the nature of the local community, and a third has concentrated on administrative technicity. Meanwhile, the extension of Local Government to developing countries has stimulated comparative thinking.

the pluralism of service

Emphasis in the twentieth century, and especially after the great depression, has been placed less on the freedom left by the state to the local community than on the services rendered by government to its citizens and to the national economy. Sometimes this has involved a consideration of Local Government as a means of action; but often it has not.

The central government as major partner in the economy has set a pattern into which local government bodies, like everyone else, have had to fit. The Keynesian economics of the 1930s, for example, with its call for the countercyclical timing of public works, had obvious implications for central guidance of public capital outlay, which included investments by local government bodies among others.

The central government as wholesale promoter of services to citizens has been interested in devolving responsibility on to "independent" retailers, but has become to a considerable extent ideologically indifferent as to who or what they might be. Local government bodies became only one among a number of possibilities, as may be illustrated from practically every typically modern service.

The concept of a national minimum level of living, evolved at the turn of the century by Charles Booth and the Webbs, involved government action to place a floor beneath the level of consumption. So far as this implied minimum income security, it was reinforced by Keynesian conceptions: what had initially looked like income-transfer in the interest of social justice was now seen as another stabilizer of the national economy. In the search for means of achieving these purposes, autonomous social insurance funds were developed. In the English-speaking countries it was increasingly taken for granted that, in a mobile economy, these should be national and bureaucratic and have as little as possible to do with the local community. On the European continent, on the other hand, the localism of Bismarckian Germany was maintained, and it was taken for granted that national rein-surance of federated local funds would be equally effective, with the result that the major local government units were paralleled with one or more special-purpose income-transfer bodies, responsible to their contributor-beneficiaries. In either case, local assistance to the needy ceased to be the first line of defense against income insecurity, to such an extent that in Britain this time-honored local government service was nationalized between the wars.

The concept of a publicly provided infrastructure of physical facilities, regardless of whether initiative in the rest of the economy were public or private, coincided with the needs of automobile traffic and the possibilities of hydroelectric power and long-distance power-trans-mission to shift the emphasis from local to national highway, power, and water-control systems. Here again it was taken for granted in the English-speaking countries that if government wished to devolve the administration of infrastructural facilities on to a financially autonomous body, this might well be a centrally established public "authority" or public corporation, or a national public holding company with regional subsidiaries, and that this need have no direct organic connection with the local communities served. On the part of some practitioner theorists, such as Herbert Morrison in England and Marshall Dimock in America, the newly invented public corporation became in the 1930s the object of a cult reminiscent of that attached to Local Government only a half-century earlier, and to some extent replacing it. It even provided the means by which a Labour government after World War II undid by nationalization the municipal socialism that had dominated the British scene during the generation before World War I. Here again, however, the European continent showed itself less etatist and more respectful of local communities if not of Local Government as such, in its effort to decentralize decision-taking responsibility and to satisfy local interests. It became normal, for example, for French chambers of commerce, statutorily responsible to the business community of all or part of a departement, to be granted concessions for ports, airports, and other facilities, which they could operate on a self-financing nonprofit basis in the interest of profit-making business; and this, like the local social security funds, was justified on the ground that local users had a community of interest which they ought to be free to express and serve through a common local organ. Continental European administrative jurisprudence safeguarded to local government units and other local public bodies the right to become shareholders in mixed enterprises, to which many important services of more-than-local scope, such as river-basin development, were entrusted. When regional planning boards were set up by a national government on the European continent, local government units were given representation alongside clientele groups.

Thus in respect of economic facilities and services, "territorial decentralization" to elective local bodies was now being everywhere supplemented by decentralization to autonomous bodies based on limited function or restricted clientele, with the former prevailing in the English-speaking countries and the latter on the European continent. A similar trend was to be found in the operation of such social programs as health, welfare, and housing.

In no major developed country in the North Atlantic

region has a comprehensive health service been organized through Local Government. In Britain medical care came to be nationally organized through autonomous regional boards and special-purpose local executive committees, while in the United States the systematic provision of health facilities and services began to emerge mainly through national support for sponsor-instituted private agencies; and in both countries the medical profession encouraged the bypassing of Local Government. Only preventive medicine has normally depended on Local Government.

In providing noneconomic welfare services of a personal kind, most branches of a new North American social work profession condoned a widespread assumption of responsibility by sponsor-instituted local private agencies; and when the federal government felt driven to enlist the cooperation of the poor themselves in breaking the cycle of poverty, it relied on nonprofit corporations whose boards were drawn one-third from beneficiary target-area groups and one-third from concerned civic organizations. Social service in France has been provided largely in connection with beneficiary-managed local income-transfer funds, social centers, or labor welfare committees. Only in the case of "wards of the state" have social work services normally depended on Local Government in Britain, France, or the United States.

When governmental action was required to help create new communities in Britain, it took the form of the designing and construction of a planned community by a public "new towns corporation"; only for its subsequent operation was Local Government made responsible. In the United States it took the form of federal underwriting of private credit in ways that might bypass metropolitan and municipal planning and administration but had the support of the organized private interests involved; in urban renewal, it required consultation with the people of the neighborhood involved; and, in public housing, it sought ways of transferring responsibility from Local

Government to other public authorities and to private operators.

The only professional service that has continued to be to a major extent supplied through elective local government bodies is the one that had its origins during their heyday in the nineteenth century—education. Yet in most American localities this service continues to be devolved on a special-purpose elective agency, while in England it is devolved on a partly-coopted special-purpose statutory committee of the general-purpose local-government body, both of which arrangements are believed to facilitate the influence of an increasingly autonomous teaching profession. Moreover, in sharp contrast with nineteenth-century practice, there has arisen a marked tendency for the central government in France and the United States to aid the education of children who attend schools provided not only by Local Government but also by diocesan institutions.

The civil rights movement in the United States, in its nonviolent and violent local lawbreaking and its judicial and legislative federal lawmaking, has been directed largely against Local Government as unequal provider of schools, protector of persons and property, regulator of business, and employer of labor.

Behavioral scientists, in search of a field of observation of manageable dimensions, have studied community power structure and decision-making as never before, but only to demonstrate implicitly the distance between the issues raised by local influentials and those requiring national policy-making, or the extent to which local decisions may relate to the application of national programs.

In spite of all of its newness and complexity, the service state of the twentieth century is thus precipitating its own distinctive pattern of local administration. Decentralization is certainly practiced on a grand scale and in many forms. Local government bodies are far from forgotten; but they have had to take a relatively modest place in a new world of financially autonomous statutory

funds, authorities and corporations, sponsor-instituted
voluntary agencies, beneficiary associations both compulsory and voluntary, and professional bodies, to
sometimes sit alongside these newcomers and rivals on
mixed enterprises and joint planning boards, and to
submit to national standards of equitable service. One
can no longer, however, as in Lorenz Stein's day, draw a
line between some of these as private and others as
public bodies; for public and private alike may perform
public functions by agreement with the government or
with resources provided by it. Nor can one say, with
Toulmin Smith, Lieber, or Gneist, that they practice
self-government in the sense of nonintervention by higher
authority; for the powers they enjoy are limited by the
funds put at their disposal, and these are never uncon-
ditional. The standards to which they must adhere are
set for them from above, even though they may go
through the form of voluntarily making them their own.
They may not always be required or compelled to accept
aid or render service of a given standard; but they may
have no moral alternative in the light of accepted ideals
of professional service as well as the expectations of
consumers. We are back in a world of myriad intermediary bodies; yet not just intermediary bodies cushioning
the impact of sovereign power on subject persons, but
rather intermediary bodies that transmit services from a
multifaceted center to all the localities in the land. Here is
a certain pluralism; not, however, the pluralism of autonomous bodies moving each in its own orbit, but that of
bodies that take their direction from a central focus of
policy and power.

the developed urban community

The multiplication of governmental activities and in-
strumentalities has been accompanied by a change in the
scale and nature of urbanization. In all earlier ages, this
had meant a densely concentrated urban minority in the
midst of a widely scattered rural majority. It had also

implied that this urban minority needed and could have certain common facilities and services that were either not needed or not practicable among the rural population; and it had raised their life to a succession of high peaks, one of which was the nineteenth century, with its invention of corporate structures, both public and private, through which capital could be invested in mechanized water supply, sewage disposal, light and power, and passenger transport.

This same process of mechanization, however, enabled the formerly restricted city to break its bounds. In the technologically developed countries it led, by the mid-twentieth century, to a new urbanization, in which for the first time the majority of the population was now urban and the minority rural, but in which the urban population was dispersing or deconcentrating while the rural population was acquiring urban standards.

In the presence of a dynamically evolving society and economy, new methods of social study and new forms of social theory emerged. "Communities" were studied that were based on subjective feelings of having something in common, even though they had not become dependent on common services and facilities or acquired corporate status, and that might have natural leaders though they had no officially selected representative organs. A community became a psychological pattern or behavioral microcosm rather than a formal structure. American rural sociologists who opened up this path found a precursor in Toennies. A school of urban sociologists from the 1920s studied the urban population in its natural group-ings and the social controls by which its inherent disor-ganization was mitigated. The Lynds by the 1930s reached a concept of local power structure of which local public authority was but one of the aspects. By the 1940s the distinction between urban and rural began to be blurred into a continuum. By the 1950s it was recognized that the spirit of mobility had made the locality into the temporary abode of outward- and upward-bound factory managers and city managers, brought in by nationwide business corporations or belonging to a nationwide profession, as well as of wage-earning commuters that came and went, living in houses that were forever being bought and sold. By the 1960s, ribbon development along a superhighway began to be thought of as giving rise to a new regional community.

Amid all this, the local government unit was but one phenomenon among many, although less of a variable than most of the others. It was in fact the most striking example of the time-lag, an institution left behind by the tide of men, seemingly destined to be supplanted and replaced by newer and more functional forms of organization. Nor would these need to be democratic; for democracy seemed to behavioralists to be but the play of pressures and interests, along with the manufacture of consent, amid a general apathy and widespread incredulity as to the existence or possibility of a public interest. While losing its function of all-purpose community organ, Local Government continued to have a special relationship to real estate values, while also continuing to cover a political subdivision, that is to say, an area in which party organization was needed for winning elections, and therefore something that was so much a part of the unwritten constitution that it could hardly be superseded.

Verhaeren's "tentacular city" that reached out into surrounding communities, Geddes' "conurbation" into which many urban entities had grown together, and the American census bureau's "standard metropolitan statistical area" formed by a nuclear city spilling over outside city limits, have all been commonplaces since the coming of electric transport. Now, however, in the motor age, came the concept of the limitless megalopolis, forever expanding, much as a boundless universe recedes into space, so that no annexation of spill over, no federation of units, and no creation of regional authorities, could keep pace with it for more than a few years—a metropolitan area that was forever becoming, with no metropolitan government that could ever be.

Within this metropolitan area came a revival of the concept of the neighborhood. First propounded in the Russell Sage survey of New York before World War I, developed by Patrick Geddes in Scotland, and adopted by Patrick Abercrombie in England during World War II, this concept had initially meant the catchment area of a primary school. It proved to be of great practical utility to city planners aiming at residential superblocks in which mothers and children would find most of the daily services they needed, without crossing major traffic arteries. Here was a community of neighbors bound together by an interest in common services. Yet this physical and social reality found no expression within the nuclear city in terms of Local Government; for such a neighborhood was seldom a ward or precinct, let alone a local government unit; nor was it always even a census tract.

From this discovery, however, came a more tolerant attitude towards those formerly rural and now suburban communities that insisted on preserving their identity, and a vague recognition that the whole metropolitan area consisted of such neighborhoods, whether they were suburban local government units or merely unorganized but socially distinctive areas within the nuclear city.

Out from all these considerations there seems to be emerging a recognition that what metropolitan man is confronted with is layer on layer of areal communities, some as small as a neighborhood and some as large as a metropolitan region, with their inhabitants dependent on common services of various and varying dimensions, each with what is for a while its optimum service area.

The practical question is how to proceed from areal theory to a governmental restructuring of metropolitan regions on the basis of residential neighborhoods grouped together in different and not necessarily constant patterns to meet their various common needs. With this might have to come a recognition that mixed enterprises are suitable forms for joint action in which local government bodies participate, in countries outside as well as on the European continent; that nuclear cities might be broken down into smaller units as well as fused into bigger ones; that a metropolitan prefect may be needed to coordinate central grants-in-aid within each metropolitan region; and that separate operating units might draw technical assistance from joint planning staffs.

Ideas such as these imply that the role of theory is not only to devise models that make it easier to understand phenomena but also to remodel the phenomena according to new shapes or patterns, and, in the case of local or other government, this necessarily implies patterns of public law. This would be in harmony with two hundred years of local government theory, and particularly with the view that one of the principal roles of central government is to determine the territorial subdivisions within which people can take civic responsibility for meeting their common needs. Behind all such theory, however, there lurks the idea that there is a certain value in people who live in the same place and are dependent on the same services having a collective organ for meeting their common needs. Local government theorists have been those that have had a place for such ideas in their scale of values.

administrativism

A characteristic twentieth-century approach to Local Government has been one that takes it for granted as a going concern within its given limits but tries to improve its efficiency. Hence a specialist literature, addressed by practitioners to practitioners. The essence of its theory is that it is best to avoid theory, avoid explicit statement of value systems, avoid declarations of faith, and think on a pragmatic and instrumentalist plane.

Of this trend there were already signs in the later nineteenth century, particularly in books in which men of one country studied Local Government in others in order to find ways and means of making their own practice more productive.

This trend became dominant in American cities from 1906, when local taxpayers' research bureaus switched the emphasis among reformers away from moral and constitutional principles to the achievement of a business efficiency that could be measured through account-keeping and fact-finding. *Efficient Democracy, Experts in City Government* and *One Best Way,* became typical book titles and chapter headings summing up the theories of those days. It was indeed from municipal management that the movement for administrative reform, under the watchwords "economy and efficiency," was soon to spread to American state and federal government. Meanwhile, this new generation of municipal reformers invented and advertised a new managerial gadgetry, more in line with current corporate practice than with American governmental tradition: first, with Woodrow Wilson's blessing, came a small "commission" to manage the municipal business, sitting as a board when formulating policy collectively and as department heads when applying it individually; and then came an appointive professional "manager" responsible to an elective council envisaged as a board of directors responsible in turn to citizen-stockholders. By the time of World War I, the American approach to municipal organization and administration, with its distinctive amalgam of governmental principle and business practice, was settling down to become an accepted, if not always consistent, body of doctrine. By the end of that war, urban cosmopolitanism could relax into isolationism: the great experience of attempting to learn from abroad was now virtually finished for a while. By the end of World War II the American way of municipal life was ready for export to Germany and Japan. A dozen professional organizations now helped American local government officials train themselves and keep abreast of one another's new experience. A host of consultant firms contracted with local government units to provide technical assistance with practical problems from the assessment of taxable property to traffic surveys. In every possible aspect of municipal government, technicity was sought; and the new administrative professionalism began to spill over into the more urbanized counties.

By the 1960s, however, the movement for intragovernmental improvement in the United States, was becoming embedded in—or circumvented by—the growing problems of intergovernmental relations. These could hardly be met by such principles as made for businesslike management within a compact corporate body. Instead, the intergovernmental demand on communication, opinion-making, incentives, negotiation, and consent created an essentially political climate before which the administrative science of the first half of the century had to confess its limitations and its ignorance. This happened, moreover, at a time when the management pattern in American business was itself changing with the absorption of local operating plants into nationwide or worldwide networks of undertakings so vast that the strict line of command was giving way to a decentralization made inevitable by bigness and complexity. It would seem not impossible, that, in local administration as in business, a way out of this imbroglio may come through the joint dependence of many local government units and other autonomous bodies on a common information processing and planning staff.

In Britain also, technicity has tended to become dominant. To some extent this has meant administrative technicity, as more attention has been given to the training of local government officials and more institutions created and textbooks published for this purpose. For the most part, however, the emphasis has been less on administrative than on professional technicity, less on general management than on specialist standards, probably because of a tendency in British local government to think in professional rather than business terms. While Ireland adapted the American manager concept, a generation passed before Britain considered it officially. The search for efficiency here remained respectful of the essential characteristics of the Benthamite pattern, in-

cluding the close working relationship between particular
council committees and the professional men who head
the various departments, and the professional guidance
and support that are given to this local combination of
elected and coopted laymen and qualified specialist by
the technically competent central ministry. This central
guidance has extended into new fields, as, for example,
the encouragement of local responsibility for the more
personal aspects of social welfare after the transfer of all
income-security services to a central authority, an encouragement that has corresponded with efforts to establish a social work profession on the North American
model. Instead of emphasis being placed on the
efficiency of each local government body taken by itself
or on the coordination of its activities, it has been placed
mainly on the techniques of partnership between central
and local government and the consequent need for policy
coordination at the center. Such power of initiative as
local government bodies have retained has been interpreted in terms no longer essentially of law but of fiscal
resources: when a local government body has set a
tax-rate to bridge the gap between central grants and the
total local cost of statutory programs, how far does it feel
able to raise this tax-rate still further in order to pay for
pioneering services that it undertakes on its own initiative?

In France it was the similar problem of central-local
relations that was dominant, with a re-study of administrative tutelage of local bodies in terms of technical efficiency, and a consequent mitigation of controls in the
case of populous communes able to afford their own
technical specialists, along with a tightening of controls
that seemed important to the national economy. Re-
gionalism ceased to be a romantic backward-looking
regret for historic territorial entities whose remains had
finally been buried at the Revolution; instead it became a
planners' tool, by providing areas for the comprehensive
programing of economic and social facilities under the
chairmanship of what were in effect regional prefects, as

well as operating units for the formulation and implementation of specific programs through regional development corporations; it was assumed, however, that the people of the region were represented as much by quasi-official and private beneficiary groups as by local government units and that the region was an administrative area rather than a new local government unit. The passage from the Fourth to the Fifth Republic confirmed the European continental tradition of the predominance of enlightened bureaucracy, strengthened it in its habits of consulting with autonomous entitites and of instituting corporate bodies on which the state could devolve operating responsibilities, and swung the balance of influence from territorial to functional bodies, away from general-purpose local government units in favor of special-purpose functional ones removed from partisan electoral control. The clash of theory was resolved by central authority; choices were made; and the changing emphasis in administrative law and legal philosophy was clear.

5

an export article

When trade, empire, and technology radiated out from
the North Atlantic among all the peoples of this planet in
the nineteenth and twentieth centuries, Local Government
went with them. It became one of the many ideas and
institutions that were to give this world a nearer approach
to cultural unity than it had ever known before.

Yet the Local Government that became an article of
export had no more sameness outside the North Atlantic
countries than in its homelands. It varied widely in conception and role, according as the political systems differed of which it was to be a part. It could be an excep-
tion to a rule of bureaucratic absolutism or centralism, or
it could be an essential and inherent part of an integrated
political system. In the latter eventuality it could play a

top-down role, involving the people in the duty of sup-
porting a system of bureaucratic constitutionalism or
democratic centralism; or it could be thought of as
playing a bottom-up role, opening doors for people to
achieve their rights, initiate development, and participate
in a pluralist dialectic.

the alien subsystem

Every political system has within it some discordant
subsystems, that it admits unwillingly and that think of
themselves as the future in gestation. This was the status
of Local Government in the Russian and Indian empires,
where it was a concession granted reluctantly and opposed continually. From the viewpoint of the bureaucratic
absolutism of the tsardom or the bureaucratic centralism
of the Indian Civil Service, it was a foreign body. The
one fought it head on. The other circumvented, neg-
lected, or starved it. In both cases the discord was to last
almost exactly fifty years and was to end in the death
—rapid in Russia and lingering in India—of the hostile or
inhospitable political system, with Local Government
playing a major role in its passing.

This approach to Local Government is one that has
often been labeled by metaphor: island, oasis, antithesis,
starting-point, or, more recently, staging area, or
launching-pad. The implications of the metaphor are
clear: Local Government may or may not stay within its
confines; it may or may not take off into a broader and
more general system of self-government.

Russia's first approximation to a local government
policy came in the 1860s when the tsar's ministry of the
interior sidetracked pressure for a parliament by issuing
administrative regulations establishing local councils.
These were to represent special interests rather than the
public at large, the governorate and district *zemstvos*
being elected by gentry, bourgeoisie, and peasants as
class constituencies, and the cantonal councils being
composed of peasants only. The zemstvos were to be

civil-law corporations for the purpose only of rendering and financing services to their constituents: they were to have no police powers and were to depend on the central bureaucracy for policing and enforcement. They could adopt no budget, hire no personnel, and execute no program, without approval from the central bureaucracy. Certain duties of the central government were devolved upon them, with the zemstvos obliged to provide barracks and prisons, while the cantonal councils were to collect revenue and maintain police while doing nothing on their own initiative. If members broke the regulations by suggesting that zemstvos correspond with one another or that zemstvos lead on to a national parliament or constitution, they exposed themselves to the risk of exile or other sanctions. In spite of all these limitations, Russian initiative found an outlet through the zemstvos, laying the foundations of a rural health service, carrying rural education to the point at which it was planned to make schooling universal during the 1920s, trading in farm supplies, and substituting monetary tax levies for the labor draft. During the Russo-Japanese war they illegally provided the army with field hospitals; after the war they were allowed to cooperate for famine relief; during World War I their union took over the state's duty of caring for the war-wounded; and it combined with the union of municipalities to contract with the army to supply it with clothing and equipment. With the revolutionary emergence of armed soviets of workers, peasants, and soldiers in 1917, the zemstvos were democratized by adjunction of representatives of these councils, as the first step towards sharing in the most nearly total collapse and replacement of a regime that have occurred in modern times.

A countrywide policy of Local Government began on the Indian subcontinent as soon as the British government abolished the East India Company and assumed direct responsibility for government after the mutiny of 1856. It began not as a matter of principle, but as a financial expedient; not with the right to local elections,

but with the duty of local taxation. A central government
unable to pay its own way resolved to distinguish between central and local benefits and to allocate the cost
accordingly. Urban municipalities were authorized initially as a means of obliging the urban population to meet
most of the cost of urban policing and subsequently as a
way of having them pay for education, sanitation, and
medical assistance. Rural boards were authorized in
connection with the introduction of a land revenue sur-
charge for local police, education, sanitation, or roads.
The execution of this policy was left to provincial governors and district officers. Except in the bigger cities
and one province, these preferred representation by
appointment to representation by election; they preferred
representation of special interests—economic, religious,
ethnic, or caste—to representation by area; they preferred to see a local body controlled from within by an
official as chairman, rather than to see a nonofficial
elected chairman; they preferred not to have English-
style functional committees capable of holding officials
accountable for their administration; they treated local
funds fed from land revenue surcharges as part of their
administrative budgets, and in many localities levied
them themselves without involving a rural board in what
to them was an administrative procedure; and they preferred associating a few of the larger landowners with the
district officers as advisers to promoting local councils
nearer to the people. Municipal corporations pleased
themselves as to what extent they would carry out even
their mandatory functions; lower-level rural boards were
free to do nothing, or not even come into existence,
unless voluntary contributions were obtainable; and all
local bodies remained poor, through unwillingness to
institute a local housetax in addition to surcharges on the
centrally-imposed land revenue. To this set of unevenly
distributed practices, the name "local *self*-government"
became attached, because of its prevalence among
contemporary British romantics and because the term
"local government" was then used in British India to

mean provincial administration. There were Indians, however, who valued and used these limited opportunities for responsible participation in administration; and the day was to come when a generation of middle-class leaders who had served their apprenticeship in municipal politics and administration would be ready to take literally the term Local Self-government, as meaning that this was where self-government was to begin. This happened at the end of World War I, when liberal British rulers conceded the right of direct election of provincial legislatures, along with the transfer to elected provincial ministers of responsibility for such "nation building" functions as Local Government. With that decision, Local Government ceased to be a controlled nuisance in a bureaucratic world, to enter into the maelstrom of nationalist politics.

In both the Russian and the Indian empires this experience became associated with surprisingly similar political philosophies. In both, the achievements of Local Government were due to local initiative and were effected in the teeth of distrust by the centralized bureaucracy. In both they became linked with a cult of civic voluntarism and a belief in revolution welling up peacefully from below. In the one, where this spirit faced brutal opposition from fellowcountrymen both before and after the Revolution, it was to come to a violent end and to be negated by its opposite. In the other, where it overcame halfhearted repression from expatriates, it was to have an opportunity to grow into an integral part of a new political system.

The two countries even shared to some extent a common literature. The extreme and uncompromising philosophies of refugees from tsarist Russia became part of the inspiration of Gandhi. Michael Bakunin's Young Hegelian negation of state and society by community and Peter Kropotkin's natural history of *Mutual Aid* among workers and peasants found a practical but equally extralegal echo in a village reconstruction movement that made Indian nationalism unique.

the integrative subsystem

The fifty years following World War I have been marked by two major revolutionary currents—the communist and the anticolonial—that have remade the political systems of three quarters of mankind. These have used Local Government as a vital element in the new pattern. At a time when its fire has been largely spent in the developed countries of the North Atlantic, it has burned as never before in the rest of the world. It has there become an essential part of the repatterning of political and other institutions; the structuring of nation-states; the process of institutional development that has everywhere pre-ceded economic development; and the reallocation of power in ways that help or hinder the take-off into other aspects of self-sustaining growth.

The political systems that have emerged have been markedly different in their emphases. Some have stressed centralization of power, while others have accepted or promoted an untidy pluralism of interacting poles of in-fluence. The role and status of Local Government have been largely determined by this general and overriding pattern. One way this has made for involvement from above; the other way it has spoken of development from below. One way it has thought of local as well as central government as the input of which all economic and social change is the output: the other way it has thought of a multiplicity of social inputs of which governmental policy both central and local is the output. One way it has stressed local duties; and the other, local rights. What-ever the political system, Local Government has tended to share in its general character, and to be used as one of the forces that make towards a general harmony in its operation. It becomes valued as one of the integrative elements in the system as a whole, regardless of whether its strength comes from a centralist call for popular participation or from a localist cult of grass-roots initia-tive.

The centralizing approach to Local Government
reached the developing world for the first time during not
this but the previous half-century. Local Government and
constitutionalism were part of Japan's road to modernization in the Meiji era. During the 1870s the whole
structure of local administration was made over along
standard European continental lines, with a pyramid of
artificial geographical subdivisions, a hierarchy of prefectoral, subprefectoral, and mayoral representatives of
central authority, deliberative bodies at the prefectoral
and communal levels, landtax and surcharges paid in
cash for use at local levels, a periodic staff meeting of
prefects, and a Home Ministry to manage the machine.
During the 1880s preparations were made to cap the
administrative reforms by imperial grant of a constitutional charter instituting a parliament. As part of this
process, Ito, who had served as Home Minister, visited
Berlin and Vienna in 1882–83 to study bureaucratic
constitutionalism with assistance from Stein and Gneist;
and the last of the thirty items on his agenda was
"systems of local administration." After his return, he was
helped in the drafting of the imperial constitution by
Hermann Roesler, the government's technical assistance
consultant on public law, who had written on the role of
autonomous entities in administration. Yamagata, who
was one of Ito's successors as Home Minister and took
Prussia as his civic and military model, hired a student of
Gneist's and instructor at Berlin, Albert Mosse, on a
five-year technical assistance contract (1886–91) to help
codify the local administration regulations, so that these
might be a fait accompli before the meeting of the first
parliament, an essential part of the unwritten constitution,
outside the scope of the written constitution or of parliamentary legislation. This codification was effected
along the lines of the Prussian variant of the European
standard model. Thus internal checks were instituted by

having inner "councils" with some appointive members
as well as elective "assemblies"; by making these into
collegial executives in urban municipalities; by trying to
build up the rural subprefecture, like the Prussian *land-
kreis;* by distinguishing sharply between locally-admin-
istered central duties, such as policing and education,
and locally-decided services of local benefit that can be
carried out without compulsion; by grouping electors by
social class; and by drafting them to serve as honorary
officials. As in Gneist's teaching, constitutionalism and
legalism were here combined with "self-government at
the emperor's command." Democratic conceptions of
power legitimized by derivation from a sovereign people
were rejected. Elective bodies were to be limited by
imperial prerogative, not the reverse. Local Government
was to be a school of public service and patriotic duty.
There was nothing historical or traditional about this,
except the spirit of service, legitimation by grant from the
emperor, and preservation at the bottom of the hamlet as
a private corporate *section de commune;* but it was to
help keep state and society together and thus ensure
progress with stability. This model was destined to be
exported to other countries under Japanese rule, including Korea and Taiwan where it took root. It was also
borrowed by China in the last year of the Manchu dy-
nasty, although in the 1920s Sun Yat-sen was still having
to envisage a period of political tutelage, while subpre-
fects would set up effective administration in their *hsien*
and win the confidence of the people before calling on
them to participate in elections.

The pattern evolved in the Soviet Union in the dozen
years after 1917 and later exported has much in common
with this Prussian-style approach. Lenin's heritage of
German thinking, his study of economic development, his
research in the management and mismanagement of
revolutions, and his experience as revolutionary party
leader, seemed all to combine to convince him of the
need for what he called "democratic centralism." He was
as sure as Marx and Engels that a revolutionary party

ought to be organized from the top down by a convinced and committed leadership that mobilized subordinate organizations, and that the idea of revolution solely from below was a revolution-impeding deviation. He was sure that the centralized state was a great step forward, indispensable for the development of capitalism and for the socialist take-over. He had no respect for decentralization as such, and recognized national particularism as functional only for purposes of culture, local autonomy only for local purposes, and autonomy in general only as a stimulus to socialist competition. Yet the revolutionary take-over, the defense of the revolution against its enemies, and the continuing revolution that is government, all required that the leaders enlist the greatest possible cooperation of the people, not as masses but as organized and purposively led groups. Gneist would have felt perfectly at home in this top-down involvement of the people in the administration of the state; in the absolute supremacy of higher over lower organs; in the internal check that comes of having executive committees at every level; in recognizing citizens as equally "officials" whether they are elected or appointed; in subordinating local government organs to the next higher level of Local Government rather than to an appointive prefect; in drafting citizens to serve as unpaid activists; in linking legality with Local Government as an interacting check on arbitrary bureaucracy; and even in taking pains to prevent bourgeois interests from capturing Local Government or the state. Where Lenin's model went beyond Gneist's was in involving vast numbers of working citizens in local administration; in calling on local bodies, not only to help execute central plans but also to participate consultatively in their preparation; in buttressing the "local organs of state power" with massive "people's organizations"; and in liquidating bourgeois interests, to the point where interaction between state and society in the nineteenth-century sense had been overcome, so that Local Government was needed not as a bridge or harmonizer between these two, but simply as a subordinate articulation of state power. This found its justification in a philosophy of history; it was what was called for at a given moment in time. It was not the application of an absolute or utopian dogma or norm. Nor did it show any respect for history in the sense of a continuing heritage of historic subdivisions or traditional institutions; for every unit, from the national republics through the *oblasts* to the *rayons,* began as newly contrived machinery instituted from above. Nevertheless, this too became a model for export, to all communist-led countries of Eastern Europe and the Far East Asian mainland, after World War II.

localist initiative

Elsewhere the leaning was towards decentralization rather than centralism and towards the nonofficial as much as the official. Nowhere were these trends more marked than in India and in Africa south of the Sahara.

Different parts of the developing world have followed different approaches. By and large, the Muslim countries have preferred an authoritarian approach, tempered with central bids for local participation, due no doubt to the French, Mughal, and Ottoman traditions of administrative centralism, reinforced as these are with the tradition of respect for God-given law and authority. It is in some of the other African and Asian countries that there have been signs of another trend emerging.

One aspect of their evolution has been a movement into Local Government by way of a detour known as Community Development, an expression that has meant different things in different places. In English-speaking Africa it tended to mean a central program of adult education, emphasizing literacy, homecraft, communication of useful knowledge, and organization of clubs. In French-speaking Africa it tended to mean the central promotion of a pyramid of compulsory cooperative societies. In India it tended to be a new state agricultural extension bureaucracy reaching down to the village, with "village-level workers" supported by hundred-village "block-level" specialists trained to advise or assist them. In theory this centrally promoted program put prime emphasis on village initiative, in the nineteenth-century tradition of local self-help, the more so since in most countries it came a decade too soon to be widely used for mobilizing the population to implement specific aspects of comprehensive national development plans. It had to take as its starting-point the inherited customary leadership of the village or of the groups of which it was composed; but it had to face the problem of how far it was possible to stimulate initiative, to form new groups or to elicit a new leadership for pioneering purposes without disrupting the historic community.

In all Community Development programs, some attention was given to local public works and therefore to the local organization to effectuate them. This did not necessarily mean Local Government; but it could mean organized action by a customary village community or its customary component groups, which sometimes brought to these self-imposed tasks not only manual labor but also initiative and organizing ability. From out of the numerous writings of individual pioneers, the abundant publications of governments, and the propagation of clichés about grass roots, boot-straps, and felt-needs, there arose a conception of the leisure-time and voluntary labor of a rural neighborhood being invested in its own capital equipment. This however implied the existence of a permanent body capable of carrying on when enthusiasm had died down and maintaining the equipment created by what might be a temporary working-party; and, if this was to be a local body, it would be normal for it to be some form of Local Government. The initial Community Development cult of ad hoc working parties or customary neighborhood groups thus led unintentionally towards a new interest in formal Local Government. This was now to be promoted not only, as in utilitarian days in India, for civic education and training in responsibility, but still more because it was regarded as a means of fostering development along specific technical lines. It was envisaged essentially as a provider of the "social overheads" or "infrastructure" indispensable to economic development. The capital equipment of the locality and the personnel needed to utilize these material facilities came to be regarded as the principal concerns of Local Government in the developing countries of Africa and Asia. For these purposes new statutory bodies were instituted, steps were taken to train their elective councillors and appointive officials, specialized central technical guidance was provided, professional people were trained for public service both at the center and in the field, and here, too, an abundant literature soon emerged, for advice to governments and for the training of local government officials.

India, limited though its experience was in Local Government, produced at the turn of the century several leaders of the Indian National Congress who believed in local initiative and responsibility as strongly as any Western liberal. Most influential among them was G. K. Gokhale, who helped convince the Liberal government's royal commission on decentralization in India in 1909 that self-government and democracy ought to begin from the village and work upward. His basic reason for this belief seems to have been that it was there that the administration had to meet the people, and there therefore that the most crucial cooperation between administration and people had to occur. He seems to have been impressed also by the fact that this was the level that was "nonofficial" par excellence; for no outside official served at this level; and to him one of the essentials of Local Government was the dominance of the nonofficial. At the end of World War I, these ideas were embodied in a wave of provincial legislation, which culminated in the leadership provided by Indian provincial ministers of local self-government after responsibility for this and other nation-building services was transferred to them in 1920. Whereas such historic panchayats as survived had frequently served mainly as interpreters of gild or caste

rules or settlers of intercaste disputes, the new panchayats were statutory and villagewide, they had a tiny
income even if only from fines and fees, they were expected to function according to administrative regulations, and in some provinces a small effort was made to
promote them, as, for example, by their registrar-general
and honorary organizers at Madras; yet they were essentially permissive mutual-aid organizations rather than
bodies with delegated governmental powers, except in
Bengal where the "village union" rather than the individual "revenue village" was preferred as bottommost
unit of self-government. While the 1920s saw a great
expansion of municipal investment in secondary and
other education and public works under a middle-class
franchise and such mayors as Jawaharlal Nehru at Al-
lahabad, it was the village that became the center of
attention as the rural heart of India and the place where
change would have to occur if India were to progress.
"Thus every village will be a republic or a panchayat
having full powers," wrote Gandhi. "In this structure
composed of innumerable villages, there will be ever-
widening never-ascending circles. Life will not be a
pyramid with the apex sustained from the bottom; but it
will be an oceanic circle, whose centre will be the individual always ready to perish for the village." [6] India
became almost alone among federal states in writing
Local Self-government into the directive principles of the
federal constitution, but this with reference only to village
panchayats. Most states revamped their statutory panchayat after independence, making the village board
(gaon panchayat) responsible to a village meeting (gram
sabha), and separating the ancient judicial function from
these newer ones by setting up separate, inter-village
tribunals (panchayat nyaya). Yet these were far from
being the only village bodies. Separate from these statutory creations of the states, the all-India Community
Development program set up other ad hoc village com-

[6] *Harijan,* December 12, 1947, quoted, All-India Congress Committee
Village Panchayat Committee, *Report,* 1954, p. 13.

mittees that were to be composed of village notables and did not have to be elected. United States advisers, with their experience of an agricultural extension service working with voluntary farm bureaus, confirmed this Gandhian tradition of voluntarism and wrote of voluntary groups taking the initiative, serving as the grassroots of democracy, and perhaps ultimately growing into local government bodies. Unpaid voluntary labor by villagers (shramdan) and voluntary donation of excess holdings by larger landlords (bhoodan) were considered to have a higher moral value than compulsory labor, paid labor, or statutory land reform. Statutory and voluntary local bodies were equally "nonofficial": statutory panchayats were under no statutory obligation to discharge any function or collect any tax; and where public lands were put at their disposal by some states, it became clear that they were not even obliged to keep their corporate income-earning assets intact. Village groups of all kinds were intended primarily to provide constructive outlets for underemployed energy—opportunities for creative use of the people's *élan vital,* as Nehru suggested in his more Bergsonian moments—rather than to be organs of government. They were, in fact, too near to the people to govern them without bringing into the open the conflicts of interest that often divide a small community. When the government had to convince parliament that the Community Development program was becoming effective in creating permanent institutions through which rural people could help themselves, a study team under Balvantray Mehta proposed in 1957 the fusion of Community Development with rural Local Government in a nationwide policy of "democratic decentralization," a term that was almost immediately Indianized as *panchayat-i-raj.* Chairman (sarpanches) of village boards (panchayats) would be brought together by state statute in a *panchayat samiti* for every community development block, with the block development officer serving as secretary of this new body, and with the village-level workers (gram sevaks) serving as its employees. There was still great reluctance to establish a hierarchy of power, in which the block samiti would supervise the village panchayat or be supervised by a district advisory council (zila parishad). The emphasis was on service; and there was strong reluctance to devolve police or taxing power on the new unit. Pressure from above came less by way of local obligation than by the channeling of grants-in-aid down through the district parishad and the block samiti to the village panchayat. A system was thus achieved in which directly and indirectly elected rural local bodies earned their funds by acting as agents of the state, except to the small extent to which they received fines, levied service charges, or had income-earning corporate assets. Yet the revival of such archaic terms as nyaya and parishad conjured up memories of local sages helping people resolve their uncertainties according to conscience outside the bounds or the bonds of law. In the thinking of S. K. Dey, federal minister of community development and panchayat-i-raj, democracy meant dispersal of initiative and decentralization of thinking and action. "Democracy can survive," he wrote, "only if it is based on decentralized social action supported by a decentralized economy growing organically from the roots"; and, "if there had to be a government, it must grow from the village upwards." The individual, the family, the village, the block, the district, the state, the nation and the world family, working upwards from the bottom, would each do its utmost and then call upon the next level to do what it found to be beyond its powers. "Panchayat-i-raj as we now visualize it, will therefore mean progressive increase in competence from the ground upwards, and corresponding transfer of responsibility from the Centre to the ground. If one wishes to climb higher, one must reduce the burden of avoidable weight on his shoulders." [7] The statutory construction of panchayats was thus regarded as no mere piece of artificial machinery, but as the institutionalization of the ideas of Gandhi and the renewal

[7] S. K. Dey, *Panchayat-i-raj, A Synthesis,* (Bombay Publishing House, 1961), p. 27, 95, 124.

of the sacred tradition of the epic hero Rama who had
ruled in ayudhiya as sarpanch; and, as the minister told
the community development workers, "panchayat-i-raj
institutions can then offer patterns before which Plato's
Republic will fall into insignificance." [8]

The European empire-builders of late-nineteenth-
century Africa were so few in number that they had no
alternative but to use whatever local organization they
found. This fitted moreover with the romantic mythology
of Local Government that was then prevalent and that
colonial administrators brought with them into the
bush—that it arose spontaneously, was based on custom,
was recognized but not created by government, and was
none the worse for being aristocratic. In the hands of
Britons such as Lugard, this became Indirect Rule, under
which a hierarchy of local chiefs and councils were not
only allowed to retain their power of interpreting and
applying traditional or customary law but were also
empowered to make and enforce new bylaws, and were
obliged and paid to serve the territorial government by
enforcing its laws and collecting its taxes. In the hands of
Frenchmen such as Faidherbe and Lyautey, a separation
of powers was introduced, with village subchiefs and
their councils collecting headtax and forced labor and
maintaining order at the lowest level under the tutelage of
French officials, rather like a commune under the guidance of the subprefect, while the greater chiefs were
confined to doing justice in matters of personal law. Both
ways, this recognition of customary local organization
helped provide a foundation of local cooperation on
which to erect an inexpensive territorial administrative
framework; and wherever no local governmental structure
already existed, it was created by the bureaucracy to
simplify its task. By the end of World War II the relationship between metropolitan power and dependent
territory was changing. A British Labour minister responsible for administering grants under the new Colo-

[8] Quoted, D. C. Potter, *Government in Rural India*, (London, 1964),
p. 47.

nial Development and Welfare Act said in a dispatch to all colonial governors: "Paper plans must be translated into action and it is in the townships and villages and among the people themselves that much of this action must take place. There are many development schemes where success in whole or in part depends on the active cooperation of the people and that cooperation can best be secured through the leadership of local authorities. Without an efficient system of local government the great mass of the African population will derive only partial benefits from the monies granted for development by the colonial legislatures" (1947). Simultaneously the Fabian Society had a book prepared which argued, on the basis of British experience, that Local Government provides the indispensable administrative machinery for giving effect to people's rights to modern services as well as for bringing democracy down to the mass of the people. This then was the purpose behind the complete reorganization of Local Government that now occurred: to provide a democratically elected channel through which grant-aided services would trickle down and be supplemented. A simple system with a single layer of local government bodies was propagated, each big enough to justify a staff to carry out the new school, health, road, and market programs, but with no supervision, delegation, or pre-cepting by any other level of Local Government. If village councils were wanted, these were not to be local government units, but private or customary bodies, promoted as an aspect of Community Development. The essential function of local government bodies would be to maintain works and services; it was not essential that they engage in regulation or policing except in connection with works and services; and a new separation of powers would leave personal law to the older authorities as customary tribunals. As in Britain, administrative decisions would be made by service committees in consultation with the professional head responsible for running each service: no overall manager would be provided by government; the district officer would become an adviser; and government controls would be kept simple and be exercised on the spot. General local government codes would provide for powers over the various services to be devolved selectively by negotiation and agreement between the central and local authorities, in the hope that devolution would occur only as local bodies became adequately staffed and as they obtained the financial means to make a sizable contribution. As independence was achieved, these artificial new local government units achieved a new political importance, as a means of transcending tribal particularism and helping make a nation out of a territory. *Development from Below* was the optimistic title of an authoritative book on local government finance; but this was a concept that needed some interpreting. It meant developmental overheads at the local level, effected with cooperation of local people and supplemented from local funds, but not that major development would issue from local initiative. It left room in rural Africa, for the channeling of local energy and initiative into minor public works to occur through clan-village Community Development as well as through areal Local Government. It allowed for variation from country to country in the extent to which such national services as education and health were devolved on to local bodies, in line with differences in the availability of professionally qualified senior personnel. The French Economic and Social Development Investment Fund required a parallel development of democratically elected bodies. Those for the development of productivity and marketing were given the form of compulsory dues-paying cooperatives—the Rural Development Mutual Societies. Those at the territorial level were modeled on the general council of a French departement, until 1957, when power of administrative decision was transferred from the representative of central authority to a collegial executive responsible to what was now viewed as a legislature, so that the road was thus opened for a transition, unique in the modern world, from local government units through territorial internal self-government to national sovereignty.

In spite of all their differences in detail the Local Government institutions of India and Africa represented basically similar ideas. They stood for Local Government as a thing of value in itself, in countries that were interested in involving as many citizens as possible in the upbuilding of newly independent nations, and that valued local initiative and flexibility more than the local application of central policies and ideologies. They stressed the role of Local Government as a positive developmental agency rather than as a negative policing authority, even though in some countries this might mean investment in comparatively small-scale facilities and amenities rather than implementation of major service programs; this, however, was in keeping with the tradition of corporate patrimony that has run as an unbroken thread through the whole of modern Local Government history as though it were of its very essence. The areas chosen for the principal level of rural Local Government were not the village, but were big enough to permit the hiring of technical although not everywhere of professional personnel; and it was a matter of some indifference whether they were already established administrative areas or tribal units, or were artificial creations. The mere fact, however, that these local government units were set up meant the revolutionary creation of areal common-interest groups in countries where personal membership of tribe or caste had hitherto been more valued than territorial ties. The fact, also, that since independence they were elected by universal suffrage, opened the door to a representation that need not be confined to notables or elders. Some intentions were underlined by experience more than others, but in only one direction has the institution belied the idea that underlay it. This was in the degree of freedom that it should enjoy. For the sake of education in democracy, it was felt that it should be free to make mistakes, with the least possible bureaucratic controls; but public works required contracts that brought corruption, and jobs that balanced patronage against competence, until states decided that civic education and popular acceptance required also state scrutiny of local

budget estimates, appointments and contracts, and provision of qualified officials.

Between the true local government unit that was big
enough to set a budget, hire employees and levy a tax
and the small village community that relied on the labor
of its members, a distinction has arisen everywhere. This
has happened in India and Africa, almost as much as with
the Russian *mir* and Japanese *buraku,* the Hispanic
barrio and the Arab *qusm* or *muhallah.* This was based
partly on scale: the village community was but a neighborhood within the local government unit. The difference
came partly also from age and origin: the local government unit was new and raw, created from on high by
statute, using such innovations as elections and salaried
employment, working out of offices, and covering an area
that had not necessarily served any common purpose
previously, whereas in most though not all cultures the
village community with its elders and headman was there
from all eternity by virtue of ancestral custom, although
statute law might sometimes define or redefine some
aspect of its life, and especially its rights to property.
Behind all these other differences was one of principle:
Local Government was based on a territorial subdivision
of the state, whereas the village community was a network of face-to-face interpersonal relationships. Both,
however, were now seen to be communities united by the
common interests that come from certain aspects of
living together; both had their organs for the management
of these common interests and especially the communal
property that they could be constantly building up; and in
both of them these organs were in some way answerable
to the people. The essence both of the artificial Local
Government body and of the natural village community
was seen to be their corporate nature, the facilities they
managed, and the positive services they made available,
rather than regulatory, repressive, or more generally
negative governmental functions.

The predominantly agrarian character of the developing world has kept for its customary village community

and statutory rural local government body an importance that has now been threatened if not eclipsed in more developed countries. It has opened up by analogy the possibility of organizing its urban agglomerations also by village-like neighborhoods as the most natural way of adapting civic responsibility to the requirements and possibilities of urban life. To only a comparatively small extent, and only among the new urban middle classes, have interest groupings competed in importance with those that involve areal contiguity. These therefore are in many ways as basic in the developing world as they were in the nineteenth century in what is now the developed world. It may be that, in the developing countries too, technological change will some day shift the balance from rural to urban life and from contigual to functional groupings; but until or unless that happens, it is in the action of rural people themselves in their local communities, in the aid that comes to them from central agencies, and in the relevance of this interrelationship to the national development plan, that one must look to see how far the mass of the people are participating in—and benefiting from—all that is being attempted for the development of their national economies and the raising of their standards and levels of living.

In all previous ages it had been axiomatic that the traditional ruling society of princes and prelates and the subject population in their customary self-governing village communities formed two worlds apart under most of the civilizations that have covered this earth. Only in western Christendom, and there only since the middle ages, had a civilization arisen in which the state tended to be constitutionally articulated with local communities and other self-governing groups. What is now happening in the rest of the world is that this type of state, and with it this conception of Local Government, is now spreading into lands that were unaccustomed to it. The gulf between the ruling establishment and the subject communities is beginning to be bridged. Between the central government and the great mass of the population, this implies recognition and cultivation of intermediary bodies, and not only the mobilization of the population as an undifferentiated mass—two quite different aspects of the governmental modernization process.

The creation and maintenance of modern technical facilities and the rendering of modern professional services imply, among other measures, the subdividing of the territory into appropriate areas, the institution in each of them of an appropriate organ of Local Government, the supplying of each such organ with professionally and technically qualified personnel, and the enlistment of that organ's partnership in the many-sided task of national economic and social development.

In this new context, a new turn is inevitably given to the ancient tradition of the customarily self-governing village community, as it becomes for the first time a willing vehicle through which services may reach the people with its own aid and consent. It is uniquely fitted to reinterpret custom in terms of modern needs, to mobilize leisure-time labor, to add new facilities to the ancient patrimony of communal resources, and generally to help its people take their place in a market economy and in a professionally-serviced society. All this, however, is possible only if its corporate self-management rather than its governmental character is stressed.

The phases through which Western thinking about Local Government has passed enable us in ways such as these to understand more clearly some of the institutional problems facing the states of the developing world, and the unique solutions to which they are feeling their way. At the same time, their recent and current experience with Local Government and Community Development, the immense literature that these policies and programs have produced, and the comparisons and contrasts to which they have given rise, have helped show the significance of the varying theories and evolving emphases with which westerners have themselves approached their own distinctive but changing and multiform institution of Local Government.

bibliography

1. an intermediary body

F. F. ABBOTT, Municipal Administration in the Roman Empire, Princeton 1926.

J. ALTHUSIUS, Politica methodice digesta, Herborn (Nassau) 1603, Arnhem 1610, Groningen 1610, Herborn 1614, Arnhem 1617, Cambridge, ed. *C. J. FRIEDRICH,* 1932; English, abridged, Boston 1964.

A. BALLARD, British Borough Charters, Cambridge 1913.

J. BODIN, Six livres de la république, Paris 1576, Lyons 1577, 1578, 1579, 1580, Paris 1580, 1583, Lyons 1593, Geneva 1608, 1629, Lyons 1693, Paris 1756; Latin, Lyons 1586, Frankfort 1591, Brussels 1601,

Frankfort 1609, 1622, Amsterdam 1645; Italian, Genoa 1588; Spanish, Turin 1590; English, London 1606; abridged, Oxford 1960, Cambridge (Massachusetts) 1962.

R. BRADY, *An Historical Treatise of Cities and Burghs or Boroughs, Showing Their Original,* London 1690, 1704.

O. BREQUIGNY, "Commune," *Encyclopédie* III, 1753.

————, ed., *Ordonnances des rois de France,* XI, XII, 1777.

O. GIERKE, *Johannes Althusius und die Entwicklung der naturrechtlichen Staatstheorien,* Breslau 1880, 1909, 1913; English, New York 1939.

J. C. DE LAVIE, *Abrégé de la République de Bodin,* 1755, Paris 1793.

————, *Traité des corps politiques et de leurs gouvernements,* Lyons 1764, 1766.

N. LOSSAEUS, *De jure universitatum tractatus,* Turin 1601, Lyons 1627, Cologne 1717.

T. MADOX, *Firma Burgi, or an Historical Essay Concerning the Cities, Towns and Boroughs of England, Taken from the Records,* 1722, 1726.

J. MILTON, *Readie and Easie Way to Establish a Free Commonwealth,* London 1660, 2nd edition 1660, editor *TOLAND* 1698 etc.; New Haven, editor *E. M. CLARK* 1915.

C. L. DE MONTESQUIEU, *De l'esprit des loix,* Geneva 1748 etc.; English, London 1750, Worcester (Massachusetts) 1802; Nederlands, Amsterdam 1771; Russian, St. Petersburg 1801; Spanish, Madrid 1821.

E. PETIT-DUTAILLIS, Communes françaises, Paris 1947.

F. H. SPENCER, Municipal Origins, London 1911.

M. WEINBAUM, Incorporation of Boroughs, Manchester 1937.

2. the governmental subdivision

J. AUSTIN, Lectures on Jurisprudence or the Philosophy of Positive Law, I. The Province of Jurisprudence Determined, London 1832; completed by *SARAH AUSTIN* from *J. S. MILL's* manuscript notes, 1861–63; etc.

O. BARROT, Études contemporaines: de la centralisation et de ses effets, Paris 1861.

P. BASTID, Sieyès et sa pensée, Paris 1939.

J. BENTHAM, Constitutional Code, Vol. 1, printed privately 1827, London 1830; revised and completed from his manuscripts, in *Works,* IX (editor *J. BOW-RING*), Edinburgh 1843.

S. BRICE, Treatise on the Doctrine of Ultra vires, London 1874, New York 1875, London 1877, 1893 (editor *J. STREET*), 1930.

CARL FRIEDRICH VON BADEN, Brieflicher verkehr mit Mirabeau und DuPont, Heidelberg 1892.

E. CHADWICK, Health of Nations, London 1887.

J. A. N. CONDORCET, Vie de Turgot, Paris 1787; *Oeuvres Complètes,* 1847.

J. A. N. CONDORIET, Essai sur la constitution et les fonctions des assemblées provinciales, Paris 1789.

L. CORMENIN, De la centralisation, Paris 1842.

A. Y. DICEY, Lectures on the Relations between Law and Public Opinion in England during the Nineteenth Century, London 1905, 1914.

J. F. DILLON, Law of Municipal Corporations, New York 1872, 5th edition 1911.

P. S. DU PONT DE NEMOURS, "Mémoire sur les municipalités," August 1775; *Mémoire sur Turgot,* Philadelphia 1782, 1788.

C. B. DUPONT-WHITE, La Centralisation, Paris 1860, 1861, 1876.

————, *La Liberté politique considérée dans ses rapports avec l'administration locale,* Paris 1864 (reprinted from *Revue des deux mondes,* 1862–63).

E. HALEVY, La Formation du radicalisme philosophique, Paris 1901; English, abridged, London 1934.

F. J. C. HEARNSHAW ed., *Social and Political Ideas of Some Great French Thinkers of the Age of Reason,* London 1929.

R. DE HESSELN, Nouvelle topographie de la France, Paris 1780.

D. HUME, Essays Moral and Political, London 1741 etc. (editor *T. H. GREEN*) 1875 etc.; French, Amsterdam 1764, London 1764; German, Koenigsberg 1813.

C. E. JACOB, Law Writers and the Courts: The Influence of Cooley . . . and Dillon, Berkeley 1956.

I. KANT, Ueber den Gemeinspruch: Das mag in der Theorie richtig sein, taugt aber nicht fuer die Praxis, Koenigsberg 1793 etc.; English, Edinburgh 1891; abridged, editor *C. J. FRIEDRICH,* New York 1949.

————, *Die metaphysische Anfangsgruende der Sitten, I. Metaphysische Anfangsgruende der Rechtslehre,* Koenigsberg 1797 etc.; English, Edinburgh 1799, 1887 etc.; Latin, Amsterdam 1799 etc.; French, Paris 1837, 1853 etc.

E. LEBEGUE, Thouret, Paris 1910.

G. F. LE TROSNE, De l'Administration provinciale et de la réforme de l'impôt, Basle 1779, 1788.

J. S. MILL, Considerations on Representative Government, London 1861 etc.; French (translator *C. B. DUPONT-WHITE*), Paris, 1862, 1865, 1877; Spanish, Valparaiso 1865.

————, *Memorandum on Improvements in the Administration of India,* London 1858.

L. STEPHEN, English Utilitarians, London 1900.

E. STOKES, English Utilitarians and India, Oxford 1959.

A. R. J. TURGOT, "Fondation," Encyclopédie VII, 1757.

————, *Oeuvres postumes* (editor *MIRABEAU*), Paris 1787; *Oeuvres* (editor *DUPONT*), Paris 1809, 7:387; *Oeuvres* (editor *SCHELLE*), Paris 1922, 4:574.

H. H. WILSON, Glossary of Judicial and Revenue Terms in India, London 1853.

3. the self-governing community

H. ADAMS, Germanic Origins of New England Towns, Baltimore 1882, Johns Hopkins University studies in historical and political science, First series.

P. ASHLEY, **Local and Central Government, a Comparative Study,** London 1906; French, Paris 1920.

M. ATKINSON, **Local Government in Scotland,** Edinburgh 1904.

B. H. BADEN-POWELL, **Indian Village Community,** London 1896.

————, **Origin and Growth of Village Communities in India,** London 1899.

G. BESELER, **Volksrecht und Juristenrecht,** Leipsic 1843.

E. BOTZENHART, ed., **Steins Briefwechsel,** Berlin 1936.

J. BRYCE, **American Commonwealth,** 1888, 1899, 1910; French 1900; Spanish 1912; Italian 1913.

E. CANNAN, **History of Local Rates in England,** Westminster 1896, 1912.

T. M. COOLEY, **Treatise on Constitutional Limitations Which Rest upon the Legislative Power of the States,** New York 1868, 8th edition 1927.

A. M. EATON, "Right to local self-government," **Harvard Law Review** 13:441, 570, 638 (1900).

E. DEMOLINS, **Le Mouvement communal et municipal au moyen age,** Paris 1875.

————, **Les Libertés populaires au moyen age,** Paris 1876.

J. FISKE, **American Political Ideas Viewed from the Standpoint of Universal History,** New York 1885.

————, **Civil Government in the United States with Some Reference to Its Origins,** Boston 1890 etc.

E. A. FREEMAN, Lectures to American Audiences: The English People in Its Three **Homes,** Philadelphia 1882.

O. GIERKE, Deutsche Genossenschaftsrecht, I., Berlin 1868.

————, *II. Geschichte des deutschen Koerperschaftsbegriff,* Berlin 1873.

————, *III.* Berlin 1881; English abridgement (translator *F. W. MAITLAND*), London 1900.

————, *IV.* Berlin 1913; English abridgement (translator *E. BARKER*), Cambridge 1934, 1950, Boston 1957.

R. GNEIST,[9] *Das heutige englische Verfassungs- und Verwaltungsrecht, II. Die heutige englische Communalverfassung und Communalverwaltung, oder, Das System des Selfgovernment in seiner heutigen Gestalt,* Berlin 1860; 2nd edition *Selfgovernment: Communalverfassung und Verwaltungsgerichte,* Berlin 1870; 3rd edition 1871; extract, *Allgemeine Grundsaetze der Selbstverwaltung,* 1871; French 1867–70.

————, *Englisches Verwaltungsrecht,* Berlin 1867, 3rd edition 1883; Italian, Turin 1894–96.

————, *Verwaltung, Justiz, Rechtsweg: Staatsverwaltung und Selbstverwaltung nach englischen und deutschen Verhaeltnissen,* Berlin 1869; *Die preussische Kreisordnung in ihrer Bedeutung fuer den inneren Ausbau des deutschen Verfassungsstaates,* Berlin 1870.

[9] On Gneist's importance, see dedication by L. Stein (1865), memorial address by Gierke (1895), criticism by Redlich (1901), and tributes by Morier (1875), Preuss (1895), Lowell (1896), Webb (1922), Heuss (1926), and Halevy (1935).

G. L. GOMME, *Primitive Folk-Moots,* London 1881.

————, *Lectures on the Principles of Local Government,* Westminster 1897.

————, *The Village Community,* London 1890.

F. J. GOODNOW, *The Tweed Ring in New York City* 1888.

————, *Municipal Home Rule,* New York 1895, 1897, 1903, 1906.

————, *Municipal Problems,* New York 1897, 1911; Spanish, Buenos Aires 1901.

————, *City Government in United States,* New York 1904.

————, *Municipal Government,* New York 1909, 1919.

M. HAURIOU, *Etude sur la décentralisation,* Paris 1892, reprinted from E. LAFERRIERE ed., *Répertoire du droit administratif.*

A. HAXTHAUSEN-ABBENBURG, *Studien ueber die innern Zustaende . . . Russlands,* Hanover 1847; French, Paris 1847; English, London 1856.

P. HENRION DE PANSEY, *Des Biens communaux,* Paris 1825, 1830.

————, *Du Pouvoir municipal,* Paris 1820, 1825, 1833, 1840; Spanish, Caracas 1850.

F. C. HOWE, *The City the Hope of Democracy,* New York 1905.

F. D'IVERNOIS, *Des causes qui ont amené l'usurpation du Général Bonaparte et qui préparent sa chute,* London 1800 etc.

H. J. LASKI, ed., **One Hundred Years of Municipal Progress,** London 1935.

M. LEHMANN, **Freiherr vom Stein,** Leipsic 1903.

F. LIEBER, **Reminiscences of B. G. Niebuhr,** dedicated to Sarah Austin, London 1835; Philadelphia 1881.

——, **On Civil Liberty and Self-Government,** Philadelphia 1853, 5th edition 1911.

H. S. MAINE, **Ancient Law,** London 1861 etc.

——, **Village-Communities in East and West,** London 1871, 7th edition 1895.

R. B. D. MORIER, ed., **Cobden Club essays: Local Government and Taxation,** London 1875, 1881.

L. MICHOUD, **La Théorie de la personnalité morale,** Paris 1905, 3rd edition 1932.

J. MATTHAI, **Village Government in British India,** preface by *S. WEBB,* London 1915.

H. L. MCBAIN, **Law and Practice of Municipal Home Rule,** New York 1916.

——, **American City Progress and the Law,** New York 1918.

——, "The Doctrine of an Inherent Right of Local Self-Government," **Columbia Law Review** 16:190, 299 (1916).

E. MCQUILLIN, **A Treatise on the Law of Municipal Corporations,** Chicago 1904, 1911, 1949.

G. L. MAURER, *Einleitung zur Geschichte der Mark-, Hof-, Dorf- und Stadtverfassung und der oeffentlichen Gewalt,* Munich 1854, Vienna 1896.

————, *Geschichte der Markverfassung in Deutschland,* Erlangen 1856.

————, *Geschichte der Fronhoefe, der Bauernhoefe und der Hofverfassung,* Erlangen 1862.

————, *Geschichte der Dorfverfassung in Deutschland,* Erlangen 1865.

————, *Geschichte der Staedteverfassung in Deutschland,* Erlangen 1869.[10]

G. H. PERTZ, *Das Leben des Ministers Freiherrn vom Stein,* Berlin 1849–55.

H. PREUSS, *Gemeinde, Staat, Reich, als Gebietskoerperschaften: Versuch einer deutschen Staatskonstruktion auf Grundlage der Genossenschaftstheorie,* Berlin 1889.

————, *Entwicklung des deutschen Staedtewesens,* Leipsic 1906.

————, *Staat, Recht und Freiheit,* introduction by T. HEUSS, Tuebingen 1926.

M. RADHAKUMUD, *Local Government in Ancient India,* Oxford 1919.

J. A. ROBSON, *Development of Local Government,* London 1931, 1948.

H. ROESLER, *Lehrbuch des deutschen Verwaltungsrecht, I. Das sociale Verwaltungsrecht,* Erlangen 1872–73.

[10] History of public authority in Germany, unfinished.

A. SCHAEFFLE, Bau und Leben des socialen Koerpers, Tuebingen 1875, 1896.

F. SEEBOHM, English Village Community, London, 1883, 1884, 1890, 1920.

A. SHAW, Local Government in Illinois, Baltimore 1883.

——, *Municipal Government in Continental Europe,* New York 1895, 1901.

——, *Municipal Government in Great Britain,* New York 1895, 1901.

J. TOULMIN SMITH, Discovery of America by the Northmen, London 1839.

——, *Laws of England Relating to Public Health,* London 1848.

——, *Government by Commission Illegal and Pernicious,* London 1849.

——, *Local Self-Government and Centralization,* London 1851.

——, *The Parish,* London 1854, 1857.

——, *English Gilds* (Early English Text Society), London 1870.

L. J. STEIN, Geschichte der socialen Bewegung in Frankreich, Leipsic 1842, 1848, 1850, 1855, 1921; English, Totova, New Jersey: Bedminster Press 1965.

——, *Municipalverfassung Frankreichs,* Leipsic, 1843; French, Brussels 1859.

——, *Die Verwaltungslehre,* Stuttgart 1865, 1869, 1876, 1887.

F. TOENNIES, Gemeinschaft und Gesellschaft: Abhandlung des Communismus und des Socialismus als empirischer Culturformen, Leipsic 1887, 8th edition 1935; English (translator *LOOMIS*), New York 1940.

L. VINCKE, Darstellung der inneren Verwaltung Grossbritanniens, B. G. *NIEBUHR* ed., Berlin 1815; *M. NIEBUHR* ed., Berlin 1848.

S. and *B. WEBB, English Local Government from the Revolution to the Municipal Corporation Act: I. Parish and County,* London 1906.

———, *II–III. Manor and Borough,* 1908.

———, *IV. Statutory Authorities for Special Purposes,* 1922.

———, *The Story of the King's Highway,* 1913.

———, *English Prisons and Local Government,* 1922.

———, *English Poor-Law History,* 1927.

———, *History of Liquor Licensing,* 1903.

———, *The State and the Doctor,* 1910.

———, *Constitution for the Socialist Commonwealth of Great Britain,* 1920.

———, *Parish Councils and Village Life,* 1901, 1908.

———, *Grants in Aid,* 1911, 1920.

H. G. WELLS, Mankind in the Making, London 1903, New York 1904.

4. a local service agency

L. P. ABERCROMBIE, *Greater London Plan,* London 1945.

W. H. ALLEN, *Efficient Democracy,* New York 1907.

D. N. CHESTER, *Central and Local Government,* London 1951.

F. A. CLEVELAND, *Chapters in Municipal Accounting,* New York 1909.

R. H. CONNERY et al., *Federal Government and Metropolitan Areas,* Cambridge 1960.

R. A. DAHL, *Who Governs?* New Haven 1961.

P. DOUEIL, *L'Administration locale a l'épreuve de la guerre,* Paris 1950.

J. A. FAIRLIE, *Essays in Municipal Administration,* New York 1908.

————, *Local Government in Counties, Towns and Villages,* New York 1906, 1920.

J. W. FESLER, *Area and Administration,* Alabama 1949, 1964.

P. GEDDES, *Cities in Evolution,* London 1915.

A. H. HANSEN et al., *State and Local Finance in the National Economy,* Cambridge 1941.

F. HUNTER, *Community Power Structure,* Chapel Hill, 1953.

A. MAASS, ed., *Area and Power,* Glencoe 1959.

A. W. MACMAHON, **Administration of Federal Work Relief,** Chicago 1941.

R. C. MARTIN, **Grass Roots,** Alabama 1964.

R. MASPETIOL and *P. LAROCQUE,* **La Tutelle Administrative,** Paris 1930.

H. MORRISON, **Socialization and Transport,** London 1933.

L. MUMFORD, **Culture of Cities,** New York 1938.

P. A. SOROKIN and *C. C. ZIMMERMAN,* **Principles of Rural-Urban Sociology,** New York 1929.

M. R. STEIN, **Eclipse of Community,** Princeton 1960.

A. SYED, **Political Theory of American Local Government,** New York 1966.

D. WALDO, **The Administrative State,** New York 1948.

W. H. WICKWAR, **The Social Services,** with *MARGARET WICKWAR,* London 1936, 1946.

——, **The Public Services,** London 1938.

——, **Antipoverty in South Carolina,** Columbia 1967.

——, "Regional and Community Administration," **University of South Carolina Governmental Review,** 10 (2), Columbia 1968.

Y. WILLBERN, **The Withering Away of the City,** Alabama 1964.

R. C. WOOD, **Suburbia,** Boston 1959.

5. an export article

G. AKITA, *Foundations of Constitutional Government in Modern Japan,* Cambridge (Massachusetts) 1967.

F. ALBI, *Derecho municipal comparado del mundo Hispanico,* Madrid 1955.

A. S. ALTEKAR, *Sources of Hindu Dharma,* Sholapur 1952.

D. E. ASHFORD, *National Development and Local Reform,* Princeton 1967.

R. BRAIBANTI, *Administration and Economic Development in India,* Durham 1963.

T. T. CH'U, *Local Government in China under the Ch'ing,* Cambridge (Massachusetts) 1962.

R. DELAVIGNETTE, *Les Vrais chefs de l'empire,* Paris 1941, 1945; English, London 1950.

S. K. DEY, *Panchayat-i-raj, a Synthesis,* Bombay 1961.

J. S. FURNIVALL, *Netherlands India,* Cambridge (England) 1939.

————, *Colonial Policy and Practice,* Cambridge (England) 1948.

GOPALA KRISHNA GOKHALE, *Speeches and Writings,* n.d.

L. G. GOWAN, *Local Government in West Africa,* New York 1958.

A. HAXTHAUSEN-ABBENBURG, *Die laendliche Verfassung Russlands,* Leipsic 1866.

U. R. HICKS, Development from Below, Oxford 1961.

R. HINDEN, Local Government and the Colonies, London 1950.

INAYATULLAH, Dynamics of Development in a Pakistani Village, Peshawar 1963.

R. ISHII, Japanese Legislation in the Meiji Era, English, Tokyo 1958.

P. KROPOTKIN, Mutual Aid, London 1902 etc.

V. I. LENIN, Collected Works, Moscow 1927, 1960.

J. D. LUGARD, The Dual Mandate, London 1922 etc.

W. W. MCLAREN, Japanese Government Documents (Asiatic Society of Japan, *Transactions* 42:II), Tokyo 1914.

————, *Political History of Japan during the Meiji Era,* London 1916.

R. H. NOLTE, ed., *Modern Middle East,* New York 1963.

T. I. POLNER, Russian Local Government during the War, New Haven 1930.

H. TINKER, Foundations of Local Self-Government in India, Pakistan and Burma, London 1954.

W. L. TUNG, Political Institutions of Modern China, The Hague 1964.

UNITED NATIONS, Community Development in Urban Areas, New York 1961.

—————, *Decentralization for National and Local Development,* New York 1962.

P. VINOGRADOFF, Self-Government in Russia, London 1915.

W. H. WICKWAR, Modernization of Administration in the Near East, Beirut 1963.

—————, "Pattern and Problems of Local Administration in the Middle East," *Middle East Journal* 12:249, Washington 1958.

—————, "Administrative Divisions in Mainland South-East Asia," *International Review of Administrative Sciences* 25:377, Brussels 1959.

—————, "Local Authorities and Community Development," *International Union of Local Authorities Quarterly* 12:84, The Hague 1959.

—————, "One Hundred Fifty Years of Comparative Study of Local Government," *Local Government throughout the World* 1:27, The Hague 1962.

—————, "Community Development Administration in the 1960s," *International Review of Administrative Sciences,* 34:225, Brussels 1968.

R. E. WRAITH, Local Government, Lagos 1956.

—————, *Local Government in West Africa,* London 1964.

index